PREACHING
JUSTICE

PREACHING
JUSTICE

The Ethical Vocation of
Word and Sacrament Ministry

James M. Childs, Jr.

Trinity Press International
Harrisburg, Pennsylvania

Copyright © 2000 by James M. Childs, Jr.

Trinity Press International, P.O. Box 1321, Harrisburg, PA 17105
Trinity Press International is a division of the Morehouse Group.

Cover images: Isaiah, Early Christian mosaic, S. Vitale, Ravenna, Italy, Scala/Art Resource, New York. Cimabue (1240–1302), Saint Francis of Assisi, detail from Madonna with Child and Angels, S. Francesco, Assisi, Italy, Scala/Art Resource, New York. Cranach, Lucas the Elder, Portrait of Martin Luther, Uffizi, Florence, Italy, Erich Lessing/Art Resource, New York. Photograph of Howard Thurman, from the Howard Thurman Collection, Department of Special Collections, Boston University.

Cover design: Jim Booth

Library of Congress Cataloging-in-Publication Data

Childs, James M., 1939–
    Preaching justice : the ethical vocation of Word and Sacrament ministry / James M. Childs, Jr.
        p.   cm.
    Includes bibliographical references.
    ISBN 1-56338-313-6 (pbk. : alk. paper)
    1. Christianity and Justice. 2. Preaching. I. Title.
BV4235.S6 .C45   2000
241'.622 – dc21
                                                                                99-087137

Printed in the United States of America

00   01   02   03   04   05   06   10   9   8   7   6   5   4   3   2   1

For Cassie

CONTENTS

PREFACE

In 1997, on the occasion of the congregation's one hundred fifti-
eth anniversary, the people of Trinity English Lutheran Church
in Fort Wayne, Indiana, gave a generous donation to Trinity
Lutheran Seminary in Columbus, Ohio, to name a faculty chair
in honor of the late Joseph A. Sittler. Joseph A. Sittler was a
graduate of Hamma School of Theology at Wittenberg University in Springfield, Ohio, a predecessor seminary of Trinity.
Dr. Sittler went on to become a renowned preacher, theologian,
ethicist, environmentalist, and ecumenist.

It was my privilege to be elected the first Joseph A. Sittler
Professor of Theology and Ethics. This was a special thrill because Joseph Sittler had been my teacher and my friend. On the
occasion of my installation into the Sittler Chair on February 2,
1998, I delivered a paper entitled, "Preaching Justice: The Ethical Vocation of Word and Sacrament Ministry." That paper,
which was subsequently published in the Spring, 1998, edition
of *Trinity Seminary Review*, is the basis of this book. I am grateful to Trinity English Lutheran Church for their generosity and
to Trinity Lutheran Seminary for their confidence in me. I am
grateful to Joseph Sittler for his mentoring and friendship and
for the rich heritage of preaching and theological engagement
with the world that he left to us all.

While some of the many memorable things he said and wrote
will occasionally surface in the discussion, this little book is not
about Joseph Sittler's theological legacy. However, I take inspiration from his vision of preaching, his incisive ethical insight,
and his theology of the perspicuity of God's boundless and
transforming grace. Most important, I do hope that this effort reflects the sort of dedication to the church's vocation that
Dr. Sittler clearly displayed. Despite his international recogni-

tion and a distinguished career on the faculty of the University of Chicago Divinity School, he never lost touch with his roots in the church and his love and concern for his colleagues in ministry. As for his eloquence, it can only be remembered fondly; it cannot be matched.

My major focus as a theologian is Christian ethics. I approach that discipline as a pastor of the church, a preacher, and one who has been responsible for educating future pastors for more than thirty years. Therefore, my interest in matters of justice as an ethicist is also always filtered through my concern for justice in the church's proclamation and practice.

If a good case can be made for the place of justice in the gospel mission of the church, we will have made the case that it should be woven tightly into the fabric of Christian preaching.

Often consideration of justice issues is reserved for the educational ministry of the church, perhaps in the context of an adult class or forum running concurrently with other selections. There is no doubt that Christian education is an appropriate and essential venue for digging deeply into what are frequently complex subjects. Here people can be informed in greater detail. Here people can debate the issues, test out their views, be edified by interaction with other believers, and struggle with the uncertainties and ambiguities we often face in the search for just policies and social arrangements. It is hard to overestimate the value of educational ministry; it is a vital resource for the church's mission.

Though much must be said for the importance of the church's educational ministry in the quest for justice, if justice concerns are only dealt with in that setting, they will de facto be marginalized. It is the church's preaching that defines its message and its mission. It is what is preached that determines what is important. Other matters are relegated to the agenda of interest groups within the congregation or larger church. Where God's justice and our call to seek it are missing from the Sunday sermon, the social concerns committee is likely to be the loneliest committee in the congregation, with one of the smallest budgets. However, if we understand concern for justice to be intimately connected to the promises of God in Jesus

Christ, justice will be there in our preaching and prominent in the congregational mission.

In this book I intend to turn aside from the complex theoretical discussions of justice so common to the discipline of ethics. Wrestling with issues of justice theory is important work for philosophers, theologians, political scientists, and others concerned with the good of the human community. However, the concern here is, How does God's call for justice become a vital part of our preaching? and, What do we discover about justice when we attempt to preach it? How do we incorporate justice concerns into the basic Christian message? How do we engender commitment to justice among the people of God through preaching? or, Do we?

This last question, Do we? is really our first question. The church has struggled for centuries with the question of how working for justice fits into its mission. Clearly, the view I take is that the cause of justice is at the heart of the church's mission and witness. The biblical and theological basis for such a conviction is the burden of the first chapter. Here and throughout the project I will strive for strong biblical content, serious theological engagement, and a constant awareness of the liturgical resources that frame the act of preaching in the worship life of the people.

If the answer to the question, Do we? is an unqualified "Yes," then the next question is, How do we go about it? First of all we go about it by not preaching *about* it. If justice is central to the Christian life and witness, it is not simply a topic for discussion and debate; it is a Word of God to be proclaimed, a divine demand and a divine promise. Discussion and debate come after we have been addressed by the Word and captured by its power. Chapter 1 should help to make this tricky point, but chapter 2, which distinguishes preaching justice from merely moralizing about it, is equally important.

All good preaching, like all good theology, is contextual. It frames the Word of God in terms of the human situation it addresses and it frames the human situation in terms of how it is addressed by the Word of God. Therefore, the remaining chapters speak of preaching justice in dialogue with current contextual realities.

Chapter 3 poses the necessity of confronting the racism of our American context. Racism is so deep in the cultural flesh of our history that no consideration of justice in America can ignore it. Nonetheless, white Christian theologians and preachers have ignored it more often than not.

Chapter 4 draws on a dimension of the church's catholicity, its Pentecostal heritage of communicating in and through all cultures. This endowment of the Spirit is particularly important in view of the pluralistic, multicultural realities everywhere in our world. Just proclamation does not unjustly discriminate by presuming that one traditional mode of thought and expression is universal.

Chapter 5 calls upon us all to address the fact that much of the injustice in our society is a by-product of greed, in its individual and encultured manifestations.

Chapter 6 echoes the theme of chapter 4 with its emphasis on the need to deal appropriately and faithfully with the multicultural context of today. The struggle for justice means involvement with a wide variety of religious and secular perspectives. In this setting, dialogue is the way to justice and a just way to go. As an example of this dialogue we consider how preaching justice extends to the whole creation. We link Christian care for the neighbor with care for the earth, justice for humankind with justice for the whole creation.

Our final chapter brings the preacher back into the context of the church and its gospel foundations. This is the context from which we speak and for which we speak. It is our source of strength and assurance for what is often an arduous task, preaching justice and walking together with the people of God in quest of it.

Before we move forward it is important to acknowledge with gratitude others who have contributed to this project, even though they would not realize it. First of all, I want to pay tribute to my friends, Rudy and Carmella Featherstone, who are godparents to our daughter Cassie, to whom this book is dedicated. Rudy and Carmella have been an inestimable source of inspiration and understanding about justice in the name of Christ. Second, I want to offer thanks to my friend and classmate, Dick Sering, whose tireless work for justice and encouragement in this project have been a source of joy and energy. I am also grateful to the Lutheran School of Theology in Chicago, my doctoral studies home and the place where I met Joe Sittler. They share in his rich heritage along with many others. Finally, I want to thank Trinity Lutheran Seminary, President Dennis Anderson, and the faculty and board for the opportunity to pursue this project. I hope this modest effort does some justice to those who have trusted me.

ONE

FOUNDATION

*Thesis: Preaching justice is at the core
of the church's gospel proclamation.*

Toward the conclusion of the Sermon on the Mount in
Matthew's Gospel, we meet this familiar saying of Jesus:

> Everyone then who hears these words of mine and acts on
> them will be like a wise man who built his house on rock.
> The rain fell, the floods came, and the winds blew and
> beat on that house, but it did not fall, because it had been
> founded on rock. And everyone who hears these words of
> mine and does not act on them will be like a foolish man
> who built his house on sand. The rain fell, and the floods
> came, and the winds blew and beat against that house, and
> it fell — and great was its fall! (Matt. 7:24–27)

The words of Jesus and their power to transform our lives into
lives lived out in him and in his way are the solid foundation of
life in Christ. They are the foundation that cannot be eroded
by all the storms and tumult of life. They are a foundation of
"rock." Perhaps it was in Matthew's mind the same "rock" in
Jesus' statement concerning Peter's confession in 16:18, " . . . on
this rock I will build my church." The Greek for rock is the
same in both cases. Furthermore, in the Sermon on the Mount
Jesus is essentially making a claim of authority as the Christ,
the one ushering in the reign of God, an authority grounded
in his sonship. It is, of course, that authority and that sonship
that Peter confesses in 16:16.

Christ is also the rock on which we build the edifice of strong
and durable preaching. It is the good news of salvation for all

1

in Christ, the unbounded grace of God, that is the vital center of our message. Even when we preach judgment, it points us to that grace. When we seek to guide and inspire the Christian life, the power comes from that grace. The way of love we call each other to follow is a map of the path of love, which the Christ followed. Any other basis for preaching is less than that rock-solid core of the Word. It is easily blown away.

GOD'S SURE WORD AND OUR UNCERTAIN RESPONSE

The gospel of Jesus Christ has been the solid foundation on which most of Christian preaching has been built. However, what this essential message of God's good news has to do with justice, if anything at all, has drawn an uncertain response. When it comes to our neighbor's dignity, rights, and fair share of life's essential goods, what did Jesus say that we should hear and do? The answers given throughout the history of the church have varied and remain less than unanimous to this day.

Students of theology and religion during the last fifty years are likely to have read H. Richard Niebuhr's book, *Christ and Culture*. In it Niebuhr proposed to address what he characterized as The Enduring Problem. This is the age-old debate over the proper relationship between Christianity and civilization, which includes issues of Christian ethics and economic life and Christian responsibility for the social order. "The debate is as confused as it is many-sided.... So many voices are heard, so many confident but diverse assertions about the Christian answer to the social problem are being made, so many issues are raised, that bewilderment and uncertainty beset many Christians."[1]

Having noted the tenacity of this unresolved cause for debate, Niebuhr then set about the task of characterizing the different positions taken on the question throughout the history of Christian thought. His categories or types of Christian response are familiar to countless readers. Though recent critical examination has cast a shadow over the adequacy or accuracy of his grasp of certain traditions, Niebuhr's typology is still a useful heuristic device for getting at the uncertainty inherent in the diversity of views presented by the church's history.[2] It serves our limited purposes well.

Niebuhr's interest in the relationship of Christianity to culture was broader than our present focus on the church's role in issues of justice. However, Christian response to the cause of justice is certainly present as a salient feature of his discussion. He recognizes the importance of the dualistic struggle between otherworldly destiny and this-worldly responsibility. This unresolved tension, reflective of the transcendent and immanent realities of God in Christ, the Word made flesh, has been in the very marrow of Christian ambivalence about the gospel's connection to justice.

Niebuhr's "Christ against Culture" position illustrates the otherworldly bias, sometimes to the extreme. From Tertullian's antipathy to philosophy down through the monastic movement to the left wing of the Reformation, this kind of response favors separation between all that is Christian and all that is secular and historical. Our world is a sinful world whose stain easily spreads to those who become involved in its affairs. It is far more appropriate to genuine discipleship to remain uninvolved, avoiding the compromises that lurk within the entanglements of secular activities.[3]

Probably the most prominent and convincing representative of this category is the great theologian Tertullian, a Roman of Carthage, whose life covered the second half of the second century and the first third of the following one. In Niebuhr's estimate, Tertullian comes close to espousing the idea that original sin is transmitted through society. One might say that culture is the medium in which the germ of sin is cultured. It follows logically that Tertullian should counsel withdrawal from as much secular occupation as possible. This admonition included rejection of political life and military service and shunning philosophy and the arts.[4] With Tertullian and others one might include here, we have a version of the Christian ethic concentrated far more on personal holiness than public justice.

At the opposite end of the spectrum is Niebuhr's "Christ of Culture" type. Here we have a concerted effort to integrate the central themes of Christian faith with the noblest aspirations of enlightened human culture. If those in the former category clung tightly to the otherworldly dimension of Christian faith, these Christians embraced its this-worldly implications. Proponents of this perspective, as exemplified by the nineteenth-century liberal theologian Albrecht Ritschl, have a clear commitment to social action in quest of justice and peace. Ritschl himself achieved a reconciliation of the tension between Christ and culture through his theology of the kingdom of God, which served as a grounding for his commitment to social transformation.

> ... the conception of the kingdom of God Ritschl ascribes to Jesus Christ is practically the same as Kant's idea of the kingdom of ends; it is closely related to Jefferson's hope for a mankind gathered into one family "under the bonds of charity, peace, common wants and common aids"; in its political aspects it is Tennyson's "Parliament of Man and Federation of the World"; it is the synthesis of the great values esteemed by democratic culture: the freedom and intrinsic worth of individuals, social cooperation, and universal peace.[5]

As one might expect and as Niebuhr demonstrated, most of the Christian tradition displays neither a wholesale rejection of culture nor an enthusiastic accommodation to it. Rather, what we see is a variety of ways in which the church has sought to strike a balance in its concern for both the otherworldly and this-worldly entailments of Jesus' person and work. This majority is represented by three different types, which, each in its own way, represent the dominant pattern that Niebuhr labeled as "Christ *and* Culture." Though differing to some degree in emphasis and theological orientation, these traditions have all attempted to distinguish but not separate Christ from human culture.

This balancing act has been a shaky one, however. The effort easily topples off the theological tightrope into a dualistic tension between Christian faith and social involvement. It is hard to stay aloft with a well-integrated and coordinated mission that points to God's transcendent future while acting out its implications for justice and the common good in the world of the present.

Lutheranism serves as a case in point for much of its history. Niebuhr identified Luther as a preeminent representative of what he called the "Christ and Culture in Paradox" position. The paradox seemingly resides in the fact that, according to Luther, we live under two modes of God's rule at one and the same time. The left-hand rule is grounded in law to govern an unruly and sinful world and the right-hand rule is established in the hearts of believers through the effluence of grace that sets us free from condemnation for a life of love.[6]

Luther set forth his doctrine of God's two modes of rule in his essay "Temporal Authority: To What Extent It Should Be Obeyed," published in 1522. The key features of his vision were then echoed in subsequent writings such as his "Commentary on the Sermon on the Mount." God's two modes of governance were appropriate to the two governments — later dubbed two "kingdoms" in the 1930s — the spiritual and the secular. As Niebuhr correctly observed, Luther had no intention of separating the two realms and expected Christians to be actively involved in both, including the quest for justice in the civil order. However, subsequent generations of Lutherans replaced the porous membrane of distinction with the solid wall of separation.

In an influential essay on Luther's two realms doctrine, nineteenth-century theologian Ernst Luthardt gave voice to the kind of dualistic interpretation that played such a dominant role for generations of Lutherans. Luthardt wrote:

> To begin with, the Gospel has absolutely nothing to do with outward existence but only with eternal life, not with external orders and institutions which could come into conflict with the secular orders but only with the heart and its relationship to God, the forgiveness of sins, etc. . . . Thus Christ's servants, the preachers, likewise have no reason to espouse these secular matters but are only to preach grace and forgiveness of sins in the name of Christ.[7]

Luthardt typified the belief that preaching should concentrate on the inner, spiritual life of the believer to the exclusion of entanglements with social and political issues. It was an outlook that was to prevail for decades and is not yet entirely dissipated.[8] In a real sense the "right hand" was determined not to know what the "left hand" was doing!

I know that years ago I, as a Lutheran seminarian, received dire warnings about preaching on matters of justice rather than sticking to justification by grace through faith. Given the regnant theological opinion in our circles that justice and justification were unrelated, those admonitions weren't surprising. This was an element in our theological education with which many of us were restive, but few of us had the experiential or conceptual tools to adequately challenge our tradition. As I look back at the sermons I preached in my student days, I naturally cringe at their immaturity of style, but more to the point, I recognize the one-dimensional character of their focus on personal faith and piety. It was not until I served as an inner-city pastor in the South during the turbulent sixties that a process of reconsideration and discovery was forced upon me by the realities of my ministry.

What Niebuhr described as a history of being torn between allegiances to Christ and to culture and what Lutherans experienced in their struggle with the dualism of left- and right-hand kingdoms, George F. Thomas saw in the problematic of properly relating love and justice. In what was one of the most widely read texts on Christian ethics in the mid-twentieth century, Thomas recounted the struggle Christian thinkers had in relating the Christian ethic of love to the concept and pursuit of justice. Some biblical theologians, he noted, believed that Jesus and the New Testament left us with no guidance on matters of justice. Others, who placed a strict interpretation on the Sermon on the Mount, went so far as to say that love and justice were virtually opposed to one another. Justice requires resistance to evil; love turns the other cheek. Still other theologians, while showing respect for the cause of justice, saw it as an approach to our relations with our neighbors that is radically different from the way of Christian love. Finally, some, who believed that Christianity is only about personal salvation, were simply unconcerned about justice; it was not considered a topic of the faith.

Parenthetically, it is interesting to observe that Thomas offered the opinion that this individualistic approach was no longer possible in the twentieth century.[9] As we shall have occasion to note in just a bit, this turns out to have been one of the least prophetic things this otherwise estimable writer had to say.

VOICES FOR JUSTICE

Thomas himself recognized that social justice and Christian love could neither be separated nor equated. The function of social justice is to ensure the common good of all people. Love has a clear interest in using this vehicle of social good as one way of expressing care and concern for the neighbor. However, as occasion provides, love is ready to go beyond the requirements of basic justice; it is ready to go the extra mile. It is generous and uncoerced. Following Reinhold Niebuhr, he sees the role of love also as one of critiquing and seeking an ever higher level of justice and remaining restive with its proximate and incomplete attainment.[10]

Reinhold Niebuhr was one of a number of twentieth-century theologians helping to lead the churches toward a lively commitment to social justice. He was more realistic about the pervasive reality of human sin and its constant threat to the establishment of justice than were his liberal predecessors in what his brother called the "Christ of Culture" mindset. At the same time, he was far more ready to affirm the partnership of love and justice in the witness of the church than many of the mainstream churches and congregations who were so reluctant to leave the safety of their personalism.

That same realism was reflected in Paul Tillich's attack on the optimism of the liberal tradition. In what he called the Protestant Principle, Tillich reasserted a central Reformation insight that we live in a fallen world whose historical transformation could never be more than fragmentary. However, despite the ambiguity of our existence, his notion of the universal scope of God's grace, operative in all the world and comprehended in the symbol of the kingdom of God, made withdrawal from involvement in the world and the cause of justice an impossibility.[11]

The universal scope of grace and its implications for the relevance of evangelical Christian faith to all spheres of life was also an important theme in the work of Joseph Sittler. Sittler wrote, "It is the nature of the gospel of redemption that all space, all personal relationships, all structures of society are the field of its energy. The gospel of the Word of God made flesh . . . the thrust of the redemptive action of God is into the structure of mankind, society, the family, and all the economic orders."[12] Sittler's concern to see the scope of grace as larger than the salvation of the individual led him to a Christology and a doctrine of grace vast enough to encompass concern for the redemption of society and the whole of nature.

Karl Barth, though assailed by his critics for having failed to integrate his theology and his social conscience, did in fact find a point of integration in his mature work, a point central to the Christian message: resurrection and the kingdom of God. When a great hope is present, as it is in the promise of the kingdom of God sealed by the resurrection victory, then small hopes for life in the immediate present are energized and pursued. These include our hopes for justice, peace, and the vindication of the poor, which we are called to seek under the positive guidance of the kingdom of God and in the hope of God's promise. Once again, in contrast to the pretense of liberal progressivism, Barth asserts that it is God, not human moral progress, who will accomplish that which we are called to seek.[13]

Figures like Niebuhr, Tillich, Sittler, and Barth, despite their theological differences, found some common themes to combat both the pretenses of liberal belief in the moral transformation of society and the quietism of so much of mainline Christianity. It was, then, Dietrich Bonhoeffer who added dramatic force to the need for Christian involvement, not only by his theology, but even more so by his martyrdom in courageous opposition to Hitler.

CHURCHES ADD THEIR VOICES

At the level of public statements, the second half of this past century has seen more and more of the church bodies of our society making a positive commitment to justice. A recent book by international economist Barend de Vries entitled *Champions of the Poor* provides a helpful synopsis of the recent positions taken by mainline denominations on the critical area of economic justice.

The best-known statement in this arena is doubtless the pastoral letter of the U.S. Roman Catholic Bishops, *Economic Justice for All*. Issued in 1986, the letter grounds its various appeals for justice and the end of oppression in the dignity of all people as persons created in the image of God. In pursuing justice, we follow the way of love to which Jesus calls us. "Love is the center of justice: *there is no justice without love*."[14] One year later some eighty Episcopal bishops issued "Economic Justice and Christian Conscience." The statement followed the Catholic bishops closely in that it stressed the necessity of the church making a moral appeal to the society. Many of the same critical justice issues were addressed as well, including urban and rural poverty, the feminization of poverty, hunger, and health care delivery.[15]

The United Methodist Church with its long history of social declarations on various justice concerns has been quite explicit in its attempts to correlate the core of the gospel with its approach to justice. We are to treat others as God has treated us, with grace. "If justice is patterned in accordance with the priority of grace, then economic goods should be produced and distributed in such a way as to enhance human well-being and self-acceptance and communal fellow feeling without asking first whether people have deserved what they receive."[16]

De Vries goes on to show how other denominations, including the Presbyterians, the United Church of Christ, the Reformed Church in America, and the Evangelical Lutheran Church in America, have all stepped up to the plate on matters of justice. His analysis of the differences and the commonalities is largely an economist's analysis, which is important, but

not for our present purposes. The overall point for our particular conversation is the fact that these church statements have
attempted to bring justice into the center ring of the church's
witness to the world.

Since we previously made Lutheranism a case in point for
the perils of dualism, it is interesting to close out this section
by visiting the consideration of economic justice currently under
way in the Evangelical Lutheran Church in America. A study
document on economic life issued for dialogue in the church
preliminary to the presentation of a social statement on that
topic included this telling statement.

> The purposes of God will not be thwarted. The dis-
> appointed promises of economic life can be faced and
> addressed. Hope emerges out of despair, life out of
> death. The coming of God's reign is not dependent on
> our achievements, but on the faithful promises of God.
> The heart of this vision provides substance and direction
> for actions and policies that can bear witness to God's
> righteousness and justice in economic life today.[17]

In comparison to past tendencies toward dualistic separation of
concerns for the world from the concerns of the faith, this is a
new departure. Here, as in Tillich and Barth, the reign of God
is the biblical and theological link between the promise of the
gospel and the quest for justice. It is to this theme that we now
turn our attention.

THE REIGN OF GOD
AND THE PREACHING OF JUSTICE

Clearly, some of the century's most prominent theologians and
the churches themselves have done a great deal to counteract
the historical tendencies to shy away from addressing justice as
a vital part of the Christian witness. However, notwithstanding
those gains, such Enlightenment progeny as the separation of
church and state, secularization, and triumphant individualism
have made a mixed marriage with the quietistic impulses of our
theological traditions to produce new offspring deeply invested

in personal spirituality but having little interest in religious claims about justice. In the words of Yale Divinity School theologian George Lindbeck, we see "multitudes of men and women who are impelled, if they have religious yearnings, to embark on their own individual quests for symbols of transcendence."[18]

In a sharp-tongued description of much of today's religious style, Larry Rasmussen has suggested that religion has become "a ready collection point for a vast array of nebulous personal yearnings and a kind of dumpster for every sort of personal problem."[19] Joseph Sittler's acerbic comment seems to be holding up: "We are tempted to regard God primarily as a God for solitude and privacy and only secondarily a God for society. We have a God for my personal ache and hurt, but no God for the problems of human life in the great world."[20]

The tradition of individualistic religion is with us in new forms. It has a new face, but the family resemblance is clear. Notwithstanding the social activism of ecumenical church organizations and the social statements of the mainline denominations, the preaching of justice in parishes where preaching is heard is as urgent a need as ever. Now, as in much of the past, justice has been a sidebar to the main text of personal salvation, where tradition is honored, or the spirituality of self-realization, where things have a more contemporary spin.

Preaching justice will be vital preaching when we clearly understand that it is at the core of the Christian proclamation of the gospel. J. Philip Wogaman in his lectures on prophetic preaching captures this understanding succinctly but powerfully. The gospel truth that God's love in Christ means God cares about each of us individually and particularly, Wogaman says, changes everything. We now see one another and ourselves in our humanity as those who are valued in Christ. "It is about justice," he says, "but not an abstract, external justice — indeed it helps to define what justice is finally all about. It is about obligation, but it is an obligation different from the requirements of external law. It is the 'obligation' to accept as a gift what God has freely given and, in our actions, to embody and truly receive the gift."[21]

When it comes to establishing that justice deserves membership in the inner circle of evangelical preaching, there is more than one way to do it. However, the one we consider here is the theological development of the strong biblical theme of the eschatological reign of God. In recent years Jürgen Molt- mann and Wolfhart Pannenberg have been most prominent in showing the central importance of this theme for understanding the gospel message of Jesus' person and work and its implica- tions for the church's work in the world. These theologians have pointed to the fact that the Bible is oriented to the promise of God's future for the world and that Jesus understood himself in terms of revealing and assuring this future reign.[22] When we come to understand what that future is all about, we realize that the promise of the gospel of Jesus Christ is more full-orbed than just the forgiveness of my sins and my personal salvation. This discovery has far-reaching consequences, then, for a more full- orbed understanding of what we include in the gospel witness of the church.

As the Bible develops its portrait of God's promised future, sealed by the victory of the resurrection over sin, evil, and death, we discover that a variety of values comprising that ultimate good result from the triumph of Easter. These values are tightly intertwined with the aims of temporal justice. These values are the focus of Christian love as it battles against all that negates them and strives for all that fulfills them. Love seeking justice in pursuit of values that are an integral part of the gospel promise of God's reign is bearing witness to its hope in that promise. The conclusion follows that love seeking justice and evangelism are indissolubly married to one another.

For the prophet Isaiah (2:2–4) the reign of God will be one of unbroken peace when swords are beaten into plowshares and spears into pruning hooks and none shall learn war anymore. When Christians engage in reconciliation at all levels of life, they anticipate the promise of peace in God's dominion. Indeed, Paul tells us in 2 Corinthians 5:19 that God, having reconciled the world to himself in Christ, has given us the call to work at this ministry of reconciliation now in anticipation of the peace- able kingdom that is to come. The work of reconciliation among people mirrors the reconciliation we have with God through the forgiveness of sins. Just as the unity and community we experience in the Lord's Supper is a foretaste of our perfect unity in the heavenly banquet, so the unity and community we seek to build through the things which make for peace anticipates the harmony of God's future.

Peace and justice are inseparable colleagues. Thus, it is not surprising that the prophet's vision of the promised future is also one of justice. In that day the Messiah will judge righteously and with equity out of concern for the poor and the meek (Isa. 11:3–5). Once again, St. Paul fills out the picture even further. In the reign of God there is equality beyond any invidious distinctions such as those between Jew and Greek, or male and female, or slave and free (Gal. 3:28). When Christians work to break down the barriers of race, gender, social class, and ethnicity, attacking the "isms" that exclude and denigrate people because of who they are, they anticipate this promised equality in the hope of its final realization. When we point a prophetic finger toward inequities in the application of the law that reflect our social prejudices and when we sue for change, we anticipate the equity with which God judges in love and righteousness.

There are key points in his ministry that demonstrate Jesus' identification of his person and his work with prophetic expectations for the reign of God. Those expectations included the triumph of life over death, the healing of infirmities, good news for the poor, and the end of oppression (Matt. 11:4–5; Luke 4:17–21). Jesus' works of healing, his empathy for those on the margins of society, his ability to face down the temptations of evil, his outreach to all sorts and conditions of people, and finally his conquest over death all point to him as the one who fulfills the prophetic hope.

When Christians uphold the sanctity of life against all that threatens it, they anticipate the triumph of life in the reign of God. When Christians not only visit the sick and comfort the suffering, but also seek to alleviate hunger and actively pursue health care for all, they bear witness to the health and wholeness of God's final future foreshadowed in Jesus' works of healing. When Christians identify with the poor and oppose all forms of oppression, they anticipate the shalom of God's rule where our final freedom from sin dissolves all oppression in the perfect freedom of life with God.

In biblical terms, the promise of God's future, revealed and secured by the Christ, is a promise for the comprehensive fulfillment of God's intention for the wholeness of the whole creation. And God does indeed will it for the *whole* creation. Isaiah's vision of cosmic harmony in the fullness of God's rule, when the wolf and the lamb shall live together and the leopard lie down with the kid (11:6–9), is given further punctuation by St. Paul. In Romans 8:21 we learn "that the creation itself will be set free from its bondage to decay and will obtain the freedom of the glory of the children of God."

The worldly ethical concerns — concerns of faith active in love seeking justice — for the spiritual and physical well-being of individuals, the common good of society, and the core of the earth point to dimensions of the gospel promise of God's reign. The church's ethical vocation is the witness of anticipation to the hopes that Jesus has implanted in our hearts. As such, this ethical vocation clearly works in tandem with the church's evangelical vocation. Both point the way to the promise. In short, preaching justice is at the core of Christian preaching. However, nothing helps to solidify a point better than a good example of this insight in action.

JUSTICE AND CONGREGATIONAL MISSION: A CASE IN POINT

In a remarkable book, *Urban Churches Vital Signs: Beyond Charity toward Justice*, Nile Harper has collected the stories of twenty-eight urban churches across the country. These are stories of how renewal and effectiveness in mission have gone hand in hand with the blending of commitments to justice into the worship life and general ministry of the congregations. The cause of justice does not supplant the gospel ministry of these congregations; it becomes a vital part of it.

One of the stories, which illustrates some of the recurrent themes of the collection, is that of Windsor Village United Methodist Church in Houston, Texas. Under the leadership of its pastor, The Reverend Kirbyjon Caldwell, Windsor Village has grown from twenty-five members in 1982 to ten thousand in 1998.[23]

Programmatically, the life of the congregation is a concrete expression of our contention that justice is central to gospel mission. The congregation enjoys a buoyant and lively worship life. This is paired with an extensive Sunday and weekday Christian education program, which includes a major emphasis on the development of prayer life. Prayer life, education, and worship life are cemented to the activism of the congregation's civic outreach. These outreach activities are too numerous to describe, but they include projects for economic and community development, health care centers, cooperative clinic programs to reach the underserved, job training, tutoring, AIDS ministry, affordable housing, advocacy, and an emphasis on members being politically active and responsible. This is only a partial list.

Worship is at the center and here the various expressions of this manifold ministry are brought together in the worshipping community. "There is a high level of expectation that the gospel will make a difference in the lives of worshippers.... Preaching is the center of worship. Sermons are biblical and practical.... Sermons deal with relationships; marriage partnership; communication; family life; social, political, economic discipline; and sacrificial giving."[24]

The key to the transformation of Windsor Village, according to Pastor Caldwell, "is understanding the Kingdom of God as a comprehensive vision that includes all aspects of human life. Biblical spirituality is not limited to the inner spiritual world. True spirituality is inclusive of people's everyday social, physical, material, and religious well-being."[25]

THE FOUNDATION OF PROMISE

We briefly return to our opening reflections on Jesus' parable. If preaching justice is to be at the core of the church's gospel proclamation, it requires a solid foundation in the gospel itself. The human pretense of this-worldliness, that we can boil the Christian message down to a program of moral transformation and inspire people to pursue it for the sake of justice, is out of touch with reality and certainly out of sync with the biblical and catholic understanding of the gospel. At the same time, the otherworldly bent of giving up on this world also fails the biblical and theological test. Both are foundations of sand that are easily eroded.

The rock is Christ and in the revelation of the Christ we are presented with the future reign of God in our every present. In Christ's victory is the assurance of this future, which God will bring to pass: "in Christ God was reconciling the world to himself..." (2 Cor. 5:19). We, in turn, are called and empowered by grace to anticipate that final future in all that we say and do. We reach out for that future because we already know what it holds.

Two

MOTIVATION

Thesis: Preaching justice is not moralizing about it.

In my student days I once had a part-time job as a banquet waiter at two different hotels in the same city. Both were elegant, both paid well, and both threw in a free meal in the kitchen for all the waiters. That is where the similarities ended. At the one hotel we worked for a maître d' that could only be described as mean spirited. He thought he could get the best work out of us if he used intimidation, invective, and fear of reprisal. By contrast, our boss at the other venue was mild mannered and rallied his corps of waiters with pep talks, encouragement, and compliments on work well done when kudos were in order.

Our menacing maître d' would stand by the entrance to the kitchen door and yell at us as we passed in and out. His degrading comments about our character and performance, punctuated with profanity, were animated by the conviction that, if given the chance, we would all cheat him and cut corners on service to the customers. This harassing made a stressful job even more so. The waiters resented him. Their incentive to give outstanding service was dampened by a lack of enthusiasm for seeing their nemesis succeed. Some worked at inventive ways to get him in trouble. Most just did what they had to in order to escape his wrath. His coercive strategy achieved a measure of compliance, but not a scintilla of commitment.

As you may have guessed, his mild-mannered counterpart provided a totally different work experience. He started by respecting us and expressing a "you-can-do-it" confidence in us.

We went about our work with pride and a desire to do a good job for him. His willingness to risk confidence and trust in us enabled us to do our best, and we did.

It seems to me that this garden-variety story of contrasting styles in wielding authority and the different results they bring raises the question of motivation. How are we motivated and what kinds of results do different kinds of motivation produce?

Coercive tactics, which begin with the assumption that persons won't correct negative behavior unless they are forced to by dire threats of consequence, may, in a way analogous to my experience as a waiter, produce compliance, but not necessarily commitment. The shame of public disapproval has been quite effective in forcing many people to stop smoking or at least to do it covertly. However, this does not mean that they have a genuine regard for the comfort of those around them or have had a conversion to a new outlook on responsible self-care. The force of law has required people to respect the civil rights of their neighbors and to provide equal access and opportunity to persons with disabilities. However, that enforced compliance does not mean that people have abandoned their prejudices or have a new empathy and respect for those with disabilities.

Ordinary experience tells us that we need the force of law and other social sanctions to assure a basic level of civil order and fundamental justice. That, we know, is needful. However, we also know that, while this needful enforcement of law and the censure of society may place persons in a situation where change is possible, it does not itself effect change. Something more is required to initiate a change of heart. At the risk of oversimplification, one suspects that that needed "extra" has to do with the discovery of self-worth and, with that, the worth of others. Without pushing the illustration too far, it seems that this is the lesson to be learned from my experience as banquet waiter.

I think Philip Wogaman has it right when he reflects on how pastoral confrontation in matters pertaining to justice, though at times even harsh, is based on the affirmation of the value of the person. It is a plea to them not to betray their own worth.

Even a stern rebuke to oppressors can be framed as good news to them. Racists, for example, have devalued themselves by treating superficial physical characteristics as most important in their humanity. In that sense the first victim of racism is the racist, because to believe in racism is to believe you have no real value as a human being. Cannot the same be said about those who cling to wealth in the face of poverty or to those who have defined their own lives in terms of power and prestige? Is it not good news to learn that life is more than that?[1]

If our common experience teaches us that motivation is best grounded in affirmation, the Bible makes that point even clearer.

SOME BIBLICAL INSIGHTS

In 1 John 4:19 we are told that we love because God first loved us. The text does not tell us that we love our neighbors because we know that if we don't, God will punish us. The appeal is to how the experience of God's love evokes our love; God loves us into loving.

In Isaiah 6 the prophet recalls the extraordinary experience of his call from God. You may recall that Isaiah saw the Lord sitting on a throne attended by seraphim who shook the temple with the voices of their praise. Isaiah was struck with fear that he, a sinner, would surely perish for having seen the Lord. But an angel took a burning coal from the altar and touched his lips, saying, "Now that this has touched your lips, your guilt has departed and your sin is blotted out" (v. 7). *Then* God asked whom shall I send, and *then* Isaiah responded, "Here am I; send me!" (v. 8). God moves first in love to affirm and make whole. At the divine touch we have a new birth and our devotion is born.

To be sure, Isaiah and all the prophets went on to speak judgment and words of judgment have not ended with the coming of the Christ to whom the prophets pointed. However, that judgment is never spoken against the people in the absence of the promise of God's love and the power that holds for them as God's people.

First of all, God's accusing word addresses us as persons whom God has lovingly created in God's very own image for a special and intimate relationship enjoyed by no other creature (Gen. 1:26). Years ago the prominent theologian Emil Brunner made the observation in his massive tome on Christian anthropology that persons are never more clearly creatures in God's image than when being addressed by God's judgment.[2] What Brunner meant was that, apart from the intimate personal relationship of the divine image, the word of judgment would either be meaningless or an expression of pure disdain and condemnation. However, made in the image of God, persons are infinitely valued by God and simply called by judgment to remember who they are. It is the abiding and indestructible relatedness of God and humanity that is the basis for obedience and, ultimately, the wellspring of its capacity.

Surely, there are few themes in Scripture that embody the reality of divine-human intimacy in a more pronounced way than the theme of covenant. It is in the context of God's steadfast covenant love that the people are called "to do justice and to love kindness" (Mic. 6:8). For Israel the law, as symbolized by the Ten Commandments, was a part of the blessing of their election, not first and foremost a source of condemnation or a ladder of virtue to be climbed in quest of God's favor. John Lochman captures this truth so beautifully by simply reminding us that the tables of the law were kept *inside* the Ark of the Covenant. Command is housed in grace. Lochman shows us the connection between the promise of the Ark of the Covenant and the new covenant of forgiveness in Christ. For the Christian life this means that God's commandments are, for Lochman, "signposts to freedom." They are a guide to life lived in the joy of freedom from the condemnation of the law.[3] This is the freedom to embrace the law as a part of our blessing.

Even the Sermon on the Mount, which seems so unyielding in its severity, is an imperative rooted in God's indicative. The Beatitudes are not the announcement of blessings bestowed as a reward for attaining the virtues they present. Rather, they are endowments, new possibilities with which the people of God are graced by the coming of the Christ in the power of God's reign.[4] If we are tempted to doubt this interpretation of the Sermon's basic orientation, then we should not forget that immediately after the Beatitudes, the similes describe the people of God first of all in the indicative: "You *are* the salt of the earth. . . . You *are* the light of the world" (Matt. 5:13–14). It is then that the imperative emerges to be salt and be light.

The imperative is progeny of the indicative. It is, Paul tells us, an exercise of life in the Spirit, life in Christ beyond the condemnation of the law, a matter of living out a life that has been graciously *given* to us (Rom. 8:1–5).

So we come full circle to 1 John 4:19. We love as we have first been loved. However, crystal clear as all this may be, we need a bit more depth and subtlety when it comes to applying the insights we have gathered thus far to the matter of preaching justice. First, some thoughts on moral appeal in general.

JUSTICE AND THE LIMITS OF MORALIZING

When we talk about advocacy for justice in general rather than preaching justice in particular, we quickly become aware of the fact that multiple strategies are needed. One, as already noted, is the necessity of having laws that safeguard basic justice in public and economic life.

There is no pretense in the enacting and enforcement of laws that those forced to obey will in every case do so out of deep moral convictions. The rule of law in society, notwithstanding its wrappings in the high-minded rhetoric of its officials and the public respectability of its institutions, operates on premises not unlike those of the hotel maître d' who badgered us so incessantly. Discounting his outward behavior, which was vulgar and off-putting, his internal rationale, like that of the law, was that many people need to be constrained by the threat of punishment. While he harassed all of us without distinction and the law intends only to punish violators, the link is still there.

Yet, even the coercive force of law is founded upon certain

positive beliefs about the dignity of all persons in society. In this regard the institutions of law in society are rather paradoxical. Though they are based on certain convictions about the dignity and rights of each individual, they also exist because of the fact that many people, if given the chance, will violate the rights of their neighbors and debase their own dignity in the process. Cynics at this point might be tempted to assert that talk of protecting human dignity is a mere philosophical cosmetic to cover over the ugly truth that law is needed simply for survival.

However, belief in some moral vision and capacity within the compass of humankind continues to prevail. It remains in a long tradition of natural law associated with Roman Catholic morality and Western philosophy and jurisprudence. In the Roman Catholic tradition, most notably developed by Aquinas, human beings are created by God with an innate ability to understand God's plan and purpose.

Theologians of the Reformation have been critical of the Catholic construal of natural law. They fear that it underestimates the impact of sin upon human reason and will and overstates human capabilities, diminishing the necessity of grace.[5]

Nonetheless, Reformation theology retained a place for a somewhat qualified and attenuated version of natural law. On the basis of Romans 2:15, where we are told that the law is written on our hearts, Luther taught a notion of natural law or "natural justice" in which he posits some ability to understand what our moral duties are.[6] The *Apology of the Augsburg Confession* followed suit by stating that persons do have a God-given capacity for "civil righteousness," for seeking justice and the common good. However, the document expresses serious reservations in that sin impairs this capacity.[7] Furthermore, Luther maintained that humanity's sense of natural law could only be awakened by the preaching of God's law.[8] These caveats notwithstanding, the avenue of appeal to some God-given natural knowledge of the good and the right remains open even if it is strewn with the potholes of human perversity.

The point of all this is that Christian theology, from Aquinas to Luther and beyond, shares with philosophy and our legal tradition a conviction, however differently nuanced, that people have some natural ability to understand what morality requires in human society. Indeed, many of these ideals are ingrained in the culture, despite our frequent fears that our ethical standards are eroding. There is a basis for making a moral appeal on behalf of justice. Moreover, it is worth doing in quest of better public policies in a pluralistic society, just as it is necessary to enact laws that foster justice and force compliance.

There is, however, a limit to what we can expect from a simple moral appeal to do justice. It is not only the limitations we face of the lingering evil in our hearts and in our institutions, which we have already mentioned. It is also the limit we encounter when we recognize that ethical principles are finally reflective of more fundamental beliefs and therefore not self-motivating. The admonition to act justly must finally be justified by an appeal to why justice fits into our ultimate convictions about the meaning of life and our hopes for the world.

I have argued that motivation is grounded in affirmation. We can now add the premise that affirmation and the meaning of moral striving are grounded in hope for and understanding of the ultimate good. We are affirmed and motivated to seek the good because the affirmation of our worth is based on that understanding of the good. At the same time, our hope for the ultimate good gives meaning to our moral striving.

In a pluralistic world there are a variety of visions of the good, some religiously founded, others humanistic, and some simply pragmatic. A simple moral appeal that fails to appreciate these underlying realities underestimates what is required to move people from compliance to conviction. It is as Paul Tillich taught us years ago. All persons have an "ultimate concern" that gives meaning to life and purpose to its projects.[9] Our vision of the good in which we find affirmation, motivation, and meaning is part and parcel of what we call our ultimate concern. The question is whether one's ultimate concern is truly "ultimate."

In chapter 1 we argued that preaching justice is at the heart of the gospel witness of the church. Justice is a part of the promise of the good to be realized in God's future revealed in Christ. In Christ we have worth and the motivation to love as we have been loved. Moreover, the love with which we have been loved is the love that reveals and bestows upon us a promise for the future in which to hope and which gives meaning to the present. Preaching justice is then a part of proclaiming this love and promise in Christ as *the* ultimate hope. Preaching justice can never be mere moral appeal! Preaching justice must do justice to the prevenient grace of the gospel in which it is couched as a promise.

We are ready now for some final and specific thoughts about preaching justice.

PREACHING JUSTICE AND THE PROBLEM OF MORALISM

Toward the end of the 1960s when the "establishment," in all its manifestations, was being assailed, theologian George Forell observed that the church was no exception. However, in the case of the church, it seems that the critics who battered the faithful with their shortcomings and irrelevance were right out of the church payrolls. Strange as it seems, church members were willing to pay for the privilege of being insulted and kept coming back for more. They were playing "Isn't it awful" at their own expense. So, Forell was prompted to ask, "Does it really do people any good to be constantly told how stupid and irrelevant they are? Is this how one best encourages them to act intelligently and with concern for present needs? . . . Are ridicule and contempt the most persuasive device to bring about changes or to encourage people to act responsibly?"[10]

We have really already answered Forell's question: It doesn't work in molding a good team of banquet waiters and it doesn't work in motivating moral commitment. However, I would have to say that since the sixties, I have continued to hear this kind of judgmental and moralistic approach more often than not when the sermon is concerned with justice. It is as though we can be shocked out of our complacency by statistics and stories that show our complicity and then shamed into a new resolve. However, it is not simply a matter of those sorts of harangues not "working." It is not simply a failure to properly motivate or justify one's moral appeal. As our earlier sortie into the biblical witness has already hinted, there is also something of central theological importance at stake.

Moralizing, the kind of lecturing that simply tells us to stop doing the wrong thing and start doing the right, is unfaithful both to the Word of God as judgment and to the Word of God as grace.

It stirs up guilt, as though guilt contained within it the chemistry to precipitate change. Thus, ironically, moralizing produces guilt in a way that hides the real depth of human sin. A true grasp of sin reveals the humanly ineradicable guilt that leads not to new beginnings, but rather to a dead end. Moralism, by working our guilt as the lever of change, misses the radical nature of God's judgment. Its admonitions betray too much faith in human possibilities. The absolute demand and the absolute judgment of God as revealed in the cross relativize humankind's noblest efforts and show us how far we are from the dominion of God.

In missing the radical absoluteness of God's judgment, moralizing about justice, with its humanistic proclivities, also misses God's absolute, radical love and mercy in Jesus Christ. By falsely overestimating our possibilities, it blinds us to our true hope in the transforming grace of God so that in the end we are left powerless.

Moralizing does not fathom the depth of sin, nor does it grasp the inexhaustibility of God's love and mercy. Therefore, moralism leads to despair over unassuaged guilt when we discover the truth of our limitations. Or it leads to the complacency of denial and self-deception, not to repentance and not to action. It is a spiritual alchemy that produces only dross.

These words about God's absolute demand from a remarkable little piece by Joseph Sittler called "The Mad Obedience God Requires" help capture what I am trying to say:

> Only the absolute demand can sensitize human beings to occasions for ethical work and energize them toward even relative achievements. And only such a demand can deliver us, in these achievements, from complacency and

pride, prevent us from making an identification of human
justice with the justice of God.... To live under the absolute demand is the only way, given the human power
of dissimulation and self-deception, to keep life taut with
need, open to God's power, under judgment by his justice, indeterminately dependent on his love, forgiveness
and grace.[11]

True preaching of justice begins and ends with God's absolute
demand and judgment and begins and ends with God's absolute grace and mercy. Moralizing about justice operates with an
illusory belief in human potential, even when it accuses and be-
rates, and ends with the existential disappointment of human
failure.

THE TRUTH OF GOD'S JUDGMENT, THE POWER OF GRACE, AND THE PREACHING OF JUSTICE

Despite what I have been saying, it also true that preaching
in many circles is usually fairly clear and often quite eloquent
about the limits of human goodness. Preaching often confronts
us with the entrenched reality of our alienation from God and
each other and with the cost of that alienation as reflected in
the agony and unspeakable brutality of the cross. In this confrontation we have been led to a grateful grasp of our utter
dependence on God's free grace.

While such a theological tack sails clear of the shoals of
moralism in its most obvious forms, it can still run aground
on the sort of individualism within which lurk the impulses
of a covert moralistic inclination. If our understanding of sin
is pegged to those transgressions of which we are particularly
ashamed and for which we are particularly grateful that God
forgives, a subtle translation of sin into a moral calculus has occurred. Though hidden from view by a genuine repentant spirit
rather than a proud one, the focus on individual transgressions
fails to fully plumb the truly tragic depths of human sin.

Effective preaching of justice, if it is to get to both God's truth about us and God's promise to us, will have to take us beyond our personal iniquities. In attempting to do so, it will also need to avoid the temptation to use examples of injustice and oppression, often far from home, as merely instances of human perversity, which illustrate an abstract doctrine of sin. We need instead to get closer to the truth of injustice as a thread of our mutual estrangement woven tightly into the fabric of our fallen humanity.

The demand upon our consciousness and our preaching is that we move to a deepened sense of our own ineluctable complicity and responsibility for injustices left untouched and acts of justice left undone. That complicity and responsibility extend to us both as individuals and as a Christian community. Helmut Thielicke's poignant words seem to fit: "So long as we are here below, we are implicated in innumerable, suprapersonal webs of guilt.... We are actors in a thousand plays which we individually have not staged, which we might wish would never be enacted, but in which we have to appear and play our parts."[12]

Our deepened sense of our inescapable involvement in the world's injustices recalls us to a deepened sense of the generosity of God's mercy and our dependence upon it. Indeed, if the motive force for our pursuit of justice on behalf of our neighbors is the experience of God's generosity toward us, it is also true that our vision of justice and preaching of justice will begin with generosity.

Effective preaching of justice will look at injustice through the lens of God's justice. God's justice begins when God hears the cry of pain and proceeds with the work of mercy. God heard the cries of the people in their captivity in Egypt (Exod. 2:23–24). God called for a jubilee to reunite impoverished and imprisoned families on the land they lost to debt (Lev. 25:8–10). This mandate for the unconditional forgiveness of debt anticipates the unconditional forgiveness of sins at the heart of justification by grace alone (Rom. 3:24), linking for us God's justice and God's justification!

In an echo of the jubilee tradition, God spoke through the prophet of Isaiah 61, proclaiming good news to the poor, freedom for the captives, and hope for the oppressed. This message of mercy and justice was then given its final and fullest meaning as a promise for God's ultimate future reign when it fell from the lips of Jesus at the inaugural address of his public ministry (Luke 4:18–19).

In the Epistle of James 5:4 we see how God is attentive to even the most mundane manifestations of injustice and the pain that it causes. The target of God's judgment is the wealthy landowners who have cheated their employees: "Listen! The wages of the laborers who mowed your fields, which you kept back by fraud, cry out, and the cries of the harvesters have reached the ears of the Lord of hosts."

Once again, with God justice begins with the cry of pain and proceeds with the work of mercy. Too often in our world, our response to the challenge of justice is not one of mercy but one of calculation; not a compassionate response to pain but a dispassionate analysis of all the barriers to change. Whether we are debating health care for the forty-three million uninsured, the needs of those who require some form of welfare, or the reality of world hunger, the tendency is not to begin with the commitment that it is morally imperative to meet such needs. Rather, our inclination as a society and as individuals is to start by enumerating the problems that stand in the way of meeting those needs. To be sure, these are large problems requiring complex action and there certainly will be difficulties along the way and reasonable debates about how to craft an effective plan. However, notwithstanding the intricacies of public policy making, we can surely preach without hesitation that there should be a plan and there should be a policy. Moreover, we can give strength to that conviction and impetus for advocacy among the people of God by pointing to the evidence of God's mercy.

However, if we have sometimes failed to preach the full extent of the judgment of God's justice, we also have often failed to preach the full scope of God's grace. If the mercy that infuses God's justice is a word spoken against our more calculating efforts, it is also a word of mercy spoken to us, which can renew us for the cause of compassionate justice. We must reiterate. Admonition and prescription without empowerment leads to self-justification and complacency or the paralysis of unrelieved guilt. Judgment and admonition get the engine racing, but without the empowering grace of God's mercy, the gearshift remains stuck in neutral.

Preaching justice that is not moralizing calls people to do God's justice in the name of a gospel that not only forgives, but also makes a new creation fraught with new possibilities. The basis of our call is that promise. The hope of our striving is in that promise and the new possibilities it creates among us and within us. Preaching justice, though it must be incisive in its judgment, involves doing better than battering people with what they aren't doing and ought to do; it involves allowing God's Word to stir up their hearts for what, by God's grace, they can do.

What I am saying is that preaching that always goes directly from sin to salvation or from cross to resurrection without ever stopping off at sanctification is missing something of critical importance. It overlooks the message of the Transfiguration event. Though we have seen the Christ in his glory on the mountaintop, for the time being we must live on the plain. We have the promise that God's Spirit is with us on that plain, graciously providing that which we need as individuals and as a body of Christ to fulfill our calling. The grace of God in Christ, which justifies, also sanctifies God's people. The good tree bears good fruit, Jesus tells us (Matt. 7:18). It is the power of God's transforming grace that makes of God's people sound trees who can bear good fruits.

Preaching justice, more than moralizing, proclaims God's grace, letting loose its power to make a people of the new creation and strengthen them in faith — God's people active in love, seeking justice. St. Paul was full of admonitions, but he was always also ready to give thanks for what God had done among the people and to assure them of the gifts they have been given for the calling to which they had been called. Even the problematic Corinthians received these reassuring words: "You are not lacking in any spiritual gift as you wait for the revealing of our Lord Jesus Christ. He will also strengthen you to the end, so that you may be blameless on the day of our Lord Jesus Christ. God is faithful..." (1 Cor. 1:7–9).

In preaching justice the indicative of God's affirmation is the wellspring of the imperative to seek justice. Though well worn, the statement of challenge to the people of God is still apt and useful: "Be what you are."

THREE

CONTEXT

*Thesis: Preaching justice in America
means addressing our racism.*

Pete Hamill's best-selling novel, *Snow in August*, tells a moving
tale of an eleven-year-old Irish Catholic altar boy in postwar
Brooklyn who forges an unlikely friendship with a rabbi. While
on his way through a vicious snowstorm to get to a Saturday
morning mass, young Michael Devlin is summoned by Rabbi
Judah Hirsch, who pleads with him to switch on the light in the
synagogue because such "work" is not permitted on the Sabbath.
This is the beginning of their warm relationship.

From this refugee of the Nazi persecutions Michael learns
Yiddish and, in return, teaches the rabbi about baseball and his
beloved Brooklyn Dodgers. As Michael enters more deeply into
his understanding of the Jewish heritage and culture, he enters
more deeply into the reality of anti-Semitism. As together they
study baseball and watch the story of Jackie Robinson, the first
black man to play in the major leagues, unfold, they both enter
more deeply into the reality of racism. Through a series of
chance events, they run afoul of the neighborhood street gang.
Together they must endure the savagery of small-time gang
violence laced with mindless prejudice and hatred.

The denouement arrives when Michael learns that he and
his mother are the targets of the local gang leader, who is en-
raged by their defiance and fearful that they will testify against
him for his various acts of violence. Michael steals into the
hospital room of Rabbi Hirsch, who has been nearly beaten
to death by members of the same gang. He convinces him to
instruct him in the secret ritual that could bring to life from

31

the earth the mythical giant, the Golem, an agent of God for justice. Michael performs the ritual and the miracle happens. Through the intervention of the Golem, justice is exacted from the gang members, the rabbi's health is restored, and hope is reborn for all.

In poignant fashion Hamill uncovers the terrible pain caused by the "isms" and cruelties that infect our lives. We are not spared by abstract discussion, but are forced by the narrative into an intimate acquaintance with the dread in which Michael and Rabbi Hirsch must live. The warmth of their friendship across the boundaries of ethnic and religious estrangement stands in stark contrast to the ever looming, destructive, sociopathic brutality of the gang. And, though there is a happy ending, it is clear that only a miracle could make it come out that way, only a supernatural intervention of God. What we view on the small screen of these two desperate lives is but one frame in a seemingly endless reel depicting the many "isms" expressive of the injustices among us, the credos of bigotry that are ideologically hardened and inherently oppressive and lethal. Here again, it seems that only a divine miracle could defeat these forces and establish justice.

All the manifestations of mean-spirited discrimination are the concern of preaching justice. However, racism is such a virulent presence in our cultural bloodstream that it deserves special mention and attention. This is not because more horrors were committed by racists than anti-Semites or more atrocities visited upon African-Americans than upon Native Americans. It is not because Jackie Robinson's pain was greater than Rabbi Hirsch's, or that African-Americans were more savaged in the South than Jews were at Auschwitz. Certainly one would not wish to discount the importance of the racist prejudice visited upon Hispanic Americans or Asian-Americans. However, it is not those sorts of comparisons that dictate the choice of our focus on racism against African-Americans. Rather, it is the fact that white-black racism is so tightly woven into the fabric of our social, political, and economic life that its effects are everywhere present even when they seem to be hidden. Indeed, one might argue with some credibility that it has provided the foundations for other manifestations of racism in our society. In the particular history of America it has become a symbol for all our prejudices.

THE PERSISTENCE OF RACISM IN CHURCH AND SOCIETY

Several decades ago, the prominent African-American theologian, James Cone, chided the theologians of the white church for not having taken the "worldly risk" of dealing with the enduring problem of color. In his judgment this failure was at the bottom of the fact that America was not producing prominent theologians. Instead, Cone argued, we were merely writing footnotes to the Germans, who, in their own contexts *had* successfully related theology to social reality.[1] His further remarks on this subject included this scathing commentary on theological education.

> The seminaries of America are probably the most obvious sign of the irrelevance of theology to life. Their initiative in responding to the crisis of black people in America is virtually unnoticeable. Their curriculum is generally designed for young white men and women who are preparing to serve all-white churches.... Most seminaries still have no courses in black church history and their faculties and administrators are largely white. This alone gives support to the racist assumption that blacks are unimportant.[2]

We are most of us familiar with the explanations one offers as to why it has been difficult to create needed changes in the situation Cone described. We bemoan the fact that there are relatively few African-American candidates "qualified for faculty positions," at least by traditional standards, and even fewer in some cases when denominational affiliation is a criterion in hiring. We note with some justification that this is a situation reflective of the perduring de facto segregation of the churches. As a consequence, gifted African-American teachers often do not feel at home in seminaries dominated by the expectations and customs of the predominantly white church. Some of the best candidates gravitate to centers of African-American theology like the Interdenominational Theological Center in Atlanta or to independent, prestigious, ecumenical schools of theology. In such venues they doubtless believe, with good reason, that they are better able to pursue their theological agenda with unalloyed integrity. Finally, as we struggle with differing opinions about how to incorporate our growing cultural diversity in the theological education of the future, we note that persons of color themselves are not all of one mind as to how this should be done. It is, then, tempting for those in the confused white majority to seize on this discord as a contributing factor in their own inability to make more progress.

However, after these and other explications have been offered up, it is impossible to escape the central truth of Cone's analysis. Certainly some progress has been made in some of our seminaries, but on balance progress among predominantly white seminaries and theological faculties has been painfully slow during the thirty years since those words were written. As Cone pointed out some years later, white seminary professors have for the most part been oblivious to the African-American experience in our history and culture. They have not explored its significance for interpreting the gospel and its ethical implications for social change. Having been in a position of power and privilege, many white theologians have failed to recognize the narrowness of their own cultural experience, because they have not had to.[3]

Writing at the beginning of this final decade of our century, Cain Hope Felder, Professor of New Testament Language and Literature at the School of Divinity of Howard University, is still able to catalogue the frustrations facing African-Americans seeking to do doctoral work in biblical studies. In what he refers to as a dominant Eurocentric approach to biblical studies, black scholars have a hard time finding a home, either as doctoral students or as teachers.[4]

Now, as the urgency of responding to our increasingly multicultural context presses upon the church and its seminaries, there is an honest recognition of the need for change and a growing number who really want to pursue it, but there is a real deficit in know-how.

In some respects the slow pace of change is not surprising given the deeply entrenched and sometimes fugitive character of racism in our society. Even when it seems that we have eliminated some of its most blatant expressions, like an adroit virus that mutates to circumvent the latest vaccine, racism continues to find new ways of infecting the bloodstream of our culture.

Derrick Bell, a prominent civil rights attorney, has defended the proposition that racism in America is permanent. Bell attacks the long-held thesis of Gunnar Myrdal's study *The American Dilemma*, that racism was an odious holdover from slavery and an "anomaly" in the liberal democratic tradition of American society. Acceptance of this thesis led to the optimistic perspective that white America wanted to abolish racism and that it had the public policy machinery to do so. Instead, Bell sides with a different view offered by Jennifer Hochschild's follow-up study of Myrdal's "anomaly thesis." Hochschild argues that racism and liberal democracy live in symbiotic relationship to one another. American society as we know it grew out of racially based slavery and is sustained by racial discrimination.[5]

As evidence of the permanence theory, Bell argues that whites have secretly bonded against blacks, even though whites at the bottom of the socioeconomic ladder share many of the same injustices as their black brothers and sisters. Racism is a deflecting power preventing class war by uniting white people across a vast socioeconomic divide. He echoes novelist Toni Morrison's conviction that, without black people as the ever present scapegoat, the country would have been Balkanized, with various immigrant groups at each other's throats. What Bell and others he draws on are saying is that our society, founded as it was with the racist presuppositions of slavery, *needs* that heritage of racism to sustain cohesiveness for the vast majority.[6]

Derrick Bell's views are hard for many people to accept. Certainly, they seem defeatist even to some African-Americans. Moreover, others would even counter that the permanence theory isn't supported by reality. A recent syndicated column offered comments that would seem to qualify as such a contrary view. Columnist Georgie Ann Geyer maintained in this particular piece that President Clinton's initiative on racism, begun in 1997, has faded away because it erroneously operated on the time-honored premise of white guilt for persistent racism. Though racism is still with us, said Geyer, the stress on "eternal white guilt and black helplessness" doesn't coincide with the new, more harmonious and just relations among the races that we currently enjoy. Citing the well-known African-American conservative Shelby Steele, Geyer went on to say that the guilt strategy produces programs like affirmative action and welfare without work that only serve to provide whites with a sense of redeeming themselves, but do little for black self-esteem and progress.[7]

It is easy to imagine a response from Bell's perspective, buttressed by statistics showing how a disproportionate percentage of African-Americans still shoulder the various burdens of poverty despite the progress of their middle-class sisters and brothers. Doubtless, there is a viewpoint that is somewhere in between. However, though we cannot resolve this kind of debate in our limited context, we should not let it deflect us from confronting the reality of racism as a shaping influence of American culture. Whether or not it is permanent, racism is clearly persistent, and it is one powerful manifestation of an enduring perversity of the human spirit that we dare never underestimate.

It is sobering, then, to note that Bell's description of matters provides a perfect example of what Reinhold Niebuhr once called "tribalism." Tribalism is the name he gave to the paradoxical and ironic fact that human beings, despite obvious marks of their unity in cohumanity, seem able to recognize a common humanity only in the unique distinguishing marks of a tribal "we-group." Those "lacking these obvious marks of tribal identity, whether racial, linguistic, cultural, or religious are treated brutally as if they were not a part of the human race." America's problem with race, Niebuhr maintained, is one vivid example of this cruel paradox.[8]

Tribalism, as Niebuhr described it, appears in its attitudes and behavior to be very much like what Cornel West, a leading African-American intellectual, has described as the need for and consumption of *existential capital*. Existential capital is the name given to those assets we desire and require as human beings to secure our needed sense of belonging and of self-esteem. There is existential capital to be gained from adherence to racist ideologies; the denigration of the one, through racist attitudes about appearance, intellect, sexuality, and character traits, lifts the self-esteem of the other.[9]

Bell's thesis that racism is permanent and its close phenomenal association with endemic tribalism and the racially permeated drive for existential capital simply serve to punctuate the assertion that racism remains lodged deep in the soul of American culture. Thus, we hear Cornel West beginning a recent book with these stunning prefatory words: "Not since the 1920s have so many black folk been disappointed and disillusioned with America."[10] For liberal whites, who devoutly hoped and thought racism was becoming a thing of the past, this kind of talk comes as an unwelcome and disconcerting revelation, often prompting denial or despair. However, it is important, as we pursue our theme of preaching justice in the context of racism, that we lift up the conviction that both denial and despair are responses from outside life in the gospel.

CHRISTIAN REALISM AND GOSPEL HOPE

Denial and despair are the symptoms of the failure of moralism in its deafness to the profound truth of what Paul Tillich called the "Law-Gospel correlation," with its blend of realism and hope. Moralism's tilt toward placing its hopes in the possibility of human moral progress tempts it to suppress some of the evidence of the intransigence of human sin in favor of celebrating the successes. In this they are a bit like the false prophets of Jeremiah 6:14 who cried "Peace, peace" when there was no peace. When that façade crumbles in the face of the facts, however, the possibility of despair becomes very real. People who have tried hard, black and white, sometimes feel like they just want to walk away.

However, entering into the reality of our problem with racism and honestly plumbing its depths is the only pathway to hope. In the novel *Snow in August*, with which we began this chapter, it took a miracle to bring about justice, a fictitious miracle borne of fantasy and legend, to be sure, but one that makes a key point. That key point is that the radical character of humanity's alienation from God and from one another requires more than humanity has to give in order for a reversal to occur.

For Christian faith and Christian preaching the miracle has occurred and its promise has been revealed.

Genesis 1:26 announces God's creation of humankind in the very image of God. The worth and dignity due all people is conferred by that special and intimate relationship with God, which is the grace of our creation and which defines our very existence. This is the foundation of the equality we share with one another.

Humankind chose to stand outside the relationship of the image of God, desirous instead of being its own god. This is the meaning of the Fall story in Genesis 3 where the serpent offers the irresistible temptation: "God knows that when you eat of it your eyes will be opened, and you will be like God, knowing good and evil" (v. 5). This is the beginning of alienation from our true selves and, therefore, from the harmony and community with God and each other intended in our creation. This is the foundation of hatred, division, and injustice, the tear in the fabric of our cohumanity so poignantly portrayed in the story of Cain and Abel (Gen. 4).

These primordial stories of biblical faith tell the truth about our condition: both our dignity and our alienation. There is a word of judgment in the story of the Fall, but a word of promise in the hope of the creation.

In the miracle of the resurrection the Christ reveals God's future as one in which the creation is fulfilled. We who are being transformed anew in the image of the Christ (2 Cor. 3:18), who is himself the image of the divine (2 Cor. 4:4), will find our fulfillment in that image in the resurrection of the dead at the arrival of God's coming reign in all its fullness. Translation: God did not quit on the creation; its promise is our hope made present in the victory of the Christ. He has run ahead of us to bring our future to us. Hope triumphs over Fall. Dignity and community are victorious over denigration and alienation.

The church is the community that celebrates and bears witness to that future in the present. We draw strength from the promise to be a community of hope. Clearly, a corollary expectation of the promise for our fulfillment in the divine image is a community in which the dignity of all is assured. In anticipation of that hope, the church today seeks to be such a community. In this we follow the lead of the very first church, launched as it was by the multicultural workings of the Spirit at Pentecost (Acts 2:7–13). It was this same Holy Spirit who led the church, as Jesus had promised, to be his witnesses across all boundaries of race and culture (Acts 1:8). By the Spirit's work through the gospel promise, the church, then and now, is called to be a *koinonia* in which "there is no longer Greek and Jew, circumcised and uncircumcised, barbarian, Scythian, slave and free; but Christ is all and in all!" (Col. 3:11, a parallel to Gal. 3:28).

The law-gospel correlation with its blend of realism and hope, as it pertains to racism, is what we are attempting to spell out in biblical terms. Cornel West appears to reflect this same blend. Despite his blunt realism, West insists that he is driven by the love of Christ to continue in hope and still to call for new alliances and partnerships among people of all races for a more just society.[11] Credible preaching of justice that addresses our racism will arise out of participation in such alliances. Indeed, the very promise of a future divine dominion in which people of all races and cultures live in community and mutual dignity suggests not only a hope but also a strategy.

CATHOLICITY AND STRATEGY

At Pentecost God gave us to one another in all our human diversity. Centuries after Pentecost we still need each other.

African-American preachers have seen the bright line con-

necting Pentecost and the church's call to seek justice against
racism. In a sermon entitled "The Hot Winds of Change,"
Samuel B. McKinney once wrote: "Pentecost is God's reversal
of Babel and the church's mission to be the sign of that reversal.
Pentecost calls for a new nation and a new people."[12] While
McKinney clearly spoke to Christians in the black church
community, the message is equally clear that a new humanity expressing our oneness in Christ on behalf of racial justice
involves the Spirit engaging all Christians. The Spirit makes
alliances! Thus, the Episcopal Church of the Messiah in De-
troit has worked for long years to deal constructively with the
racism in their community in large measure through a variety
of alliances. "Conferences, study groups, dialogues, sermons,
covenant group partnerships, shared community living arrangements, and African-American and Caucasian leaders/teachers
in residence have helped with this ongoing struggle in the
church and the surrounding community."[13]

The point of Pentecost, among other things, was to inau-
gurate the church as a "catholic" reality. Catholic refers to that
which is universal or all-inclusive. The Spirit clearly established
the church to be inclusive of all people, while yet retaining
the distinctiveness of the multitude of cultures and races that
would be a part of it. The Spirit did not inspire or enable a
single language. Rather, the apostles spoke in many tongues a
single message that would unite all people in their diversity. We
shall explore in greater depth the idea of catholicity in the next
chapter. For now I want to stress that the idea of catholicity as
inclusivity is, as one theologian has put it, "an antidote for the
poisons of prejudice and discrimination."[14] Inclusivity and the
building of alliances for racial justice are siblings born of the
same Spirit.

However, notwithstanding the birthright of Pentecost, the
church has often spurned its own catholicity. The well-worn
phrase "white flight" describes more than just the physical reality of people "moving away." Moving away is not only a matter
of geographical relocation; it is also a cultural and intellectual
decision. Fleeing the racial and ethnic diversity of changing
neighborhoods includes a tacit choice to remain monocultural

in a multicultural society. We are back to our earlier observations of James Cone's critique of theology and theological education.

Without the intellectual leadership of African-American thinkers to engender a more discerning grasp of racism and without the cultural enrichment of the African-American tradition, our society will not have the understanding requisite to build the alliances Cornel West calls for in molding a truly democratic multiracial society. If the churches of the white majority turn their backs on these resources, there will be scant chance of preaching justice with integrity and keeping faith with the promise that all are one in Jesus Christ.

However, our conversation with African-American Christianity offers more than a resource for better understanding of the race issue. The African-American preaching tradition is a theologically rich tradition from which we can all draw inspiration and instruction. We have only to look at the life and work of Martin Luther King, Jr., and his fellow leaders among the black clergy in the civil rights movement to be reminded that in African-American preaching, theology, and church life there has never been a divide between salvation and concern for justice.

"Within African-American Christianity," says James Evans, "grace conforms itself to the suffering and shame of the downtrodden, and grace transforms the quality of life itself, imputing honor in the midst of shame."[15] Remarks from a sermon by the great black preacher Benjamin E. Mays are illustrative. Mays's indictment of our long history of slavery and racism lifts up the manner in which it made black people feel like worthless nobodies. "The hopelessness and despair of so many black youths today lie in the fact that they never had dignity and worth as human beings.... Man lives best by a belief that he is somebody, God's creature, and that he has status not given to him by man but given to him by God."[16]

Evans and Mays articulate in a few words the gospel at the core of God's justice that we uncovered in the previous chapter. God's justice starts with mercy, a response to the pain of those who suffer injustice. They also make clear another truth we have emphasized. People live best and are empowered when they are affirmed. Justice begets justice! This leads directly to another important observation about the great preaching tradition of African-American Christianity.

"In the hands of skillful African-American pastors," says Robert Franklin, "preaching seeks to empower the powerless by telling the stories of God's preferential care for the disadvantaged."[17] The empowerment this preaching gives is the backbone of the political, economic, and civil rights activism so integral to the mission of the black churches.[18]

When we stand on the firm ground of realism about racism and hope in the promises of God, rather than the sandy soil of moralism, preaching justice against racism *can* lift up the successes, large and small. Certainly there are successes. There are major breakthroughs such as we have witnessed in the civil rights movement. There are racist laws that have been repealed. There are genuine displays of righteous indignation by white people in response to violence done to blacks. There is evidence of an enlarged and emerging black middle class. There are more political leaders who are African-American than we have seen before. There are authentic moments of kindness and deep friendship between people of different races that defy social patterns.

Though we can't let these victories blind us to the abiding reality of racial injustice any more than we would allow our overflowing supermarket shelves to blind us to the reality of world hunger, these are triumphs that should be celebrated. These are historic moments in which the future intrudes on the present. These are moments of eschatological grace that rekindle hope in God's promise and strengthen us as we run ahead to meet it.

FOUR

CATHOLICITY

*Thesis: Preaching justice means
just proclamation.*

"Just proclamation" does not unjustly presume that its own modes of thought are universal, to the exclusion of others. This idea has already been introduced in our discussion of racism. One manifestation of racism, we noted, is the refusal of so many white churches and theologians to take seriously the intellectual, spiritual, and experiential contributions of African-American Christianity. Now we include that observation within a larger context of concern that the church's proclamation remains open to its own God-given diversity. Just preaching will reflect the justice it preaches by being justly inclusive of this myriad of particular contributions. It will recognize that the gospel, when seen through the many lenses of our cultural and experiential diversity, is truly magnified. The catholicity of the gospel, its all-inclusive outreach and relevance, will stand out.

When something is magnified, it is also the case that we see it more clearly and we see things that we hadn't noticed before.

NEW VISIONS
AND NEW UNDERSTANDINGS

As I write this chapter, we are standing in the wake of the shocking events at Columbine High School in Littleton, Colorado. There, as most will recall, two young white students went on a rampage and killed a number of their fellow students before turning their guns on themselves. Syndicated columnist William Raspberry, an African-American, reflected on this

event and how it became an occasion for illustrating the gulf
between black and white perceptions of reality.[1]

Members of the black community noted that the parents
of the young shooters were treated with greater deference than
African-American parents would likely have been. The shooters
were referred to as members of a "clique," not a "gang," the term
most often used when African-American youth are involved. A
sign of our inbuilt racism is the fact that the incident received
such exhaustive coverage. It was in a white middle-class suburb
where such things aren't expected to happen. If it had been a
black community event, it would never have drawn so much
attention. Fear for the breakdown of families, the alienation
of youth, the availability of guns, the deficits of school programs, and TV violence all came to the fore in the discussion
of the dominant culture. Such concerns have been rejected as
contributing factors when black violence is under discussion,
however. White Americans looked at the event and saw one
thing. African-Americans looked at the same event and saw
another. The former saw a complex of social issues. The lat-
ter saw a confirmation of American racism. The key point,
which Raspberry makes, is that neither of these interpretations
is delusional; both have a piece of the truth.[2]

We need more than one set of eyes in order to see the whole
picture. The sermonic treatment of Romans 13:1–3 by a leading
African-American preacher of our time provides another case
in point. Paul's admonition in this text to be subject to the
ruling authorities as those who exercise power from God for
good has often been the basis for quietistic acceptance of the
status quo even when reform of unjust government is needed.
In the hands of our preacher, however, the emphasis shifts. The
onus is on the government to live up to God's justice, for their
power is solely from God.[3] When seen from the comfort of
the dominant culture, a conservative appreciation of respect for
government is understandable and in some measure faithful to
Paul's concerns. However, when seen from the experience of
oppression, we appreciate the need to invoke accountability to
God's just purposes through prophetic voice.

Another example that seems to fit here has to do with our

ways of thinking about race. The notion that the human family is divided into various races is an invention of the mind that has given rise to a whole realm of knowledge, which includes anthropology of race, sociology of race, physiology of racial types, and so on. On the face of it this is just another instance of the scientific study of experienced reality, presumably providing better understanding. However, such knowledge is susceptible to the abuses of power. It can be manipulated and encouraged by the dominant group for its own racist objectives. While those who have never suffered the stereotyping it can promote may think taxonomy of the races is a benign construct, those who have see it differently. W. E. B. Du Bois, the distinguished African-American thinker, saw the problem clearly. He not only indicted those who use such "scientific" knowledge to consolidate their power over others, he also attacked the adequacy of racial analysis in general.[4]

> It is easy to see that scientific definition of race is impossible; it is easy to prove that physical characteristics are not so inherited as to make it possible to divide the world into races ... that the possibilities of human development cannot be circumscribed by color, nationality, or any conceivable definition of race.[5]

To reiterate, we need more than one set of eyes to see the whole picture. This is especially true when we are looking at matters of justice. The eyes of those for whom justice is a daily issue of existential concern often possess a sharper visual acuity. The assortment of examples that follows in the next section should help to illustrate that point.

FROM INJUSTICE TO INSIGHT

Some years ago I was privileged to take part in a dialogue in Mexico City between Latin American and North American theologians on the theme of justice and justification. The focus was on how we are to understand the relationship of the two concepts in the faith and life of the church. Justification has often been separated from justice in the minds of

North American and European theologians, especially within
Lutheranism. While justice is embraced as Christian duty,
justification is God's saving work, which liberates individuals
from the bondage of sin and empowers them to seek justice.
Justification precedes the quest for justice.[6]

By contrast, their Latin American counterparts, whose theology was framed by their experience in a context of oppression,
saw justification and justice as two sides of the same coin.
Whether we are talking about individual salvation or establishing justice on earth, it is, as theologian Victorio Araya put
it, "God setting things right, bursting in with victorious force
that overcomes death and recreates life."[7]

The more traditional view taken by the North American colleagues helps preserve the gospel from becoming a program of
social transformation rather than a divine promise. The Latin
American perspective helps overcome the problem of restrict-
ing God's promise to individual justification at the expense of
pursuing justice as an integral part of God's promise. The dialogue at the conference was an exercise in the sharing of those
two visions in the hope of a more complete picture.

A number of social and political changes have occurred since
the Mexico City conference, but the lessons learned are still instructive for just preaching. This is also the case in our next
example. *The Gospel in Solentiname* by Ernesto Cardenal was
published in English in 1976. This is a collection of comments
on the Sunday gospel lessons by a group of country folk in a
remote village of Nicaragua. They spoke in their weekly discussions out of an experience of hardship under the Somoza
dictatorship.

After the publication of their thoughts on the gospel lessons,
the Sandinista revolution, which many of these Christians supported, succeeded. Now, since that time, more has changed and
the Sandinista party has been voted out of power. In the midst
of all this change in political climate, who knows what new
insights might be recorded if the Bible study continued to be
published? This alerts us to the fact that just preaching is always
a work in progress. However, the universal truth of the biblical substance remains even when the particular situation from

which it emerged has changed. Moreover, what these faithful said then remains illustrative of the fact that, when we are attentive to different cultural realities, we make new and exciting discoveries about the Word we preach. Here is a sample from one of their regular sharing sessions.

The little group was gathered to celebrate the Eucharist one Sunday morning on which the Gospel lesson under discussion was Luke 5:1–11, the account of the miraculous catch of fish. As thoughts get expressed there is certainly an appreciation shown for Peter's faith in following Jesus' command and the importance of faith in general. No one misses the prominence of the miraculous or the fact that this is an occasion for calling the disciples to be fishers of people. However, several in the community see more than these rather obvious features of the narrative.

What they see comes out of their ability to identify with the people Jesus was with in this story. They saw the fishermen and the crowds who had come to hear him as poor, working people like themselves. They saw Jesus as one in solidarity with these people and with them. Their comments, born of this intimate connection, peel back additional layers of meaning in ways that enrich our understanding of justice for the poor.[8]

> The news spread all over that he was the Messiah and the poor people came looking for him to liberate them from all their troubles and afflictions and he had pity on them and got into the boat to give them his message of liberation from there (Don José Chavarría).

However, Jesus' sensitivity to their needs and his compassion for them is channeled in a way appropriate to their being his people:

> As I see it Jesus was sorry for those people and wanted to help them. And he sees that a miracle would be a good thing, but he can't give them riches because you don't get saved from riches. You get corrupted instead. And then he orders Peter, or Simon Peter, to perform a humble miracle:

to catch fish. A miracle not of riches but of humbleness
(Tomás Peña).

As to the fear or amazement shown by the disciples, one named
Marcelino had this incisive comment:

> I think you'll always find this fear in the poor. If one fellow
> has cash, the poor think that he'll be able to order them
> around and that they can't resist. And somebody with a lot
> of education makes us feel useless too. We're always afraid
> that somebody who is more educated is going to reject us.

Then, of course, the Gospel text goes on to say that Jesus told
them, "Do not be afraid." They were not to be rejected, but to
become one with him as fishers of people.

Acceptance and inclusion as foundational to justice is prominent also in women's preaching. For women who preach out of
a feminist perspective, concern for justice is primary. This concern is then undergirded by other features that stress inclusion
and acceptance such as the use of inclusive language, allowing neither masculine nor feminine images to dominate, and
promoting a communal approach to authority.[9]

Women's preaching, says Christine Smith, "weave[s] a new
reality of justice and human wholeness."[10] It is a justice of
wholeness in life that incorporates not only a gender-inclusive,
communal vision, but also an inclusive vision that extends to
the entire natural world and respects its integrity.[11] The feminist sense of interconnectedness is a powerful vehicle for the
kind of just community we sense in the biblical image of the
body of Christ. That same strong sense of relatedness lends
force to our call to be merciful as God is merciful in our solidarity with those who are suffering. In the Bible, we have said,
justice is grounded in mercy and takes its cue from those who are
hurting. Indeed, the whole creation is hurting, Paul tells us in
Romans 8:22. The emphasis in women's preaching on environmental wholeness helps us to move beyond our anthropocentric
proclivities to consider God's love of the whole creation and our
responsibility to care for it as God does.

The experience of marginalization that women have often

shared with other groups, both inside and outside the church, can generate a keen understanding of the dramatically counter-cultural character of the gospel. Here are some salient words to that effect from a sermon by Daisy L. Machado entitled "A Powerful Gospel":

> The gospel we are needed to preach is the gospel of a new order and a new people. We are needed to proclaim, by our everyday living, that the cycle of hopelessness and death can indeed be broken, more — that it has been broken in Jesus Christ. . . . By means of a shared common life, the cycle of the world begins to be broken. By rendering impotent the power of those things that oppress and divide people — the facts of race, class, sex — the Christian community demonstrates the victory of Christ.[12]

Margaret Ann Cowden strikes a similar chord in her sermon, "Growing Pains: Learning to Relinquish in Order to Receive." She calls for

> a revival of preaching that declares to people a *new* reality, a *new* vision of ordering our life together, modeling *new* styles of partnership where people who are different than us are not merely tolerated, but loved and celebrated as true partners in mission and ministry, as persons whose *very differentness* can inform and enrich our life together.[13]

Recalling the thesis of this chapter, we might simply add to Pastor Cowden's remarks the observation that such preaching as she envisions and the Christian community it proclaims would surely lay the cornerstone for justice in just preaching.

The emphasis in these excerpts upon the church as a community living the given life, being what God has made it to be, is reflected also in the preaching of Ella Pearson Mitchell. As a woman and an African-American, she is a living embodiment of some the features shared between emerging feminist perspectives and the African-American preaching tradition.

In a sermon on the John 13 account of the Lord's Supper and of Jesus washing the disciples' feet, Rev. Mitchell chooses to set aside reflection on the theological meaning of the Lord's

Supper, even though this remains foundational. Instead her gaze
turns to the theme of servanthood evident in the actions of
Jesus. In a manner typical of African-American preaching, as
well as much of women's preaching, Mitchell preaches *out of
practice for practice.* The fact that the inauguration of the holy
mystery of the Lord's Supper is the very event at which Jesus
chooses to do this act of humble service says to Pastor Mitchell
that the Lord does not want sanctity without service. To this
she then attaches the further insight that the Lord's Table is one
to which *all* are welcome. She succeeds in helping us see that
the *sacrament* of free grace in the Eucharist yields the *sacrifice*
of service in a community of service that lives in and for the
justice of God's welcoming inclusivity.[14]

Ella Mitchell's emphasis on practice is a corollary of the
concreteness of contextual preaching characteristic of so much
of the African-American tradition. While African-American
preachers are perfectly capable of crafting an abstract doctrinal
sermon on justification or justice, they are not likely to. Henry
Mitchell puts it this way:

> The black worshipper is seeking the answers to visceral
> questions on which life itself depends. The solution of
> abstract problems can wait. The important questions are
> more pragmatic and immediate. One will have to bet one's
> life on a decision tomorrow. On what shall one stake that
> life? . . . Black preaching at its best has done this very thing
> time and again. Giving the primary emphasis to the imme-
> diate needs of people and putting the intellectual questions
> in their secondary place, the message for now has been
> proclaimed.[15]

Mitchell's comments are echoed by those of my faculty col-
league, Robert Simmons. He makes the point that African-
American worship in all its parts has historically addressed
contemporary social issues. "People of the church patiently and
often quietly await 'a word from the preacher' and a 'word from
the Lord' about the state of society and the role of the church
in social and spiritual transformation."[16]

In all these brief examples we get a glimpse of how the ex-

perience of injustice in a given community or group evokes an
insight into justice that suffuses its preaching and its apprehen-
sion of the gospel and the text. This is but another observation
that amplifies the point that we need more than one set of
eyes to see the fullness of the gospel message for all of humankind. Or, to take up the related image, when gospel is viewed
through the many cultural and experiential lenses of the church's
catholicity, it is magnified. However, how does this happen?
How is the just preaching of true catholicity fostered as well
as described?

CATHOLIC STEW

Throughout the ages we know that the church has always been
and continues to be engaged with virtually all the world's cultures. Out of that engagement have come what one might call
models of cultural catholicity. I will mention what I would consider to be three clearly discernible approaches that the church
has taken toward its global multicultural makeup. This is not
a greatly refined scholarly study of the matter. I am appeal-
ing more to the obvious. I'm going to introduce yet another
set of images, not merely for the sake of variety, but also for
their evocative potential as a means of distinguishing between
the different approaches. The images descriptive of the three
models of cultural catholicity we shall compare are these: The
Blender, The Menu, and The Stew.

The Blender Model

In a blender we take diverse ingredients, put them together, and
blend them into a liquid or a puree so they are indistinguishable
from one another. They have all been blended into one single
color and one single taste. In many organizations of our time
the desire to be totally nondiscriminatory and, therefore, treat
all justly leads to a blender type approach. There is a professed
color blindness, and gender blindness. All are the same and are
to be judged solely on their merits and contribution.

   Laudable as the intentions may be, this approach fails in at
least two critical respects. First, the emphasis on this version of

equality easily becomes an emphasis on uniformity. Uniformity suppresses the creative dynamics present in the diverse cultural and experiential makeup of the members of the organization. Something valuable is being lost here in a situation that is actually out of touch with the society in which it is operating. Second, the hidden injustice in this approach to justice is the fact that the standards of uniformity are normally established by those in power according to their own definitions of what should be normative for the organization's life and ethos. Those whose background differs from the dominant group may be unable to truly be their best. Their natural style and the perspective they bring may not be understood or appreciated if they break the pattern of uniformity.

While the blender model and its problems are readily illustrated in a variety of organizational settings, the church has certainly provided some vivid examples. Perhaps some of the most telling tales have come out of earlier efforts of European and American missionaries in African and Asian settings. Too often the missionaries simply imported their own culturally conditioned version of Christianity and expected the natives of other cultures to conform. The assumption that the worship forms, theological formulations, and organizational principles of Western Christianity were the universal and authentic expression of Christianity was a kind of cultural imperialism that we have all come to reject. Nonetheless, however misguided it may have been, it was driven by the conviction that such conformity was the bedrock of true inclusivity. It was a model of catholicity but one that suppressed the vitality of local contributions and prevented indigenous churches from coming into their own until they finally gained their independence.

The Menu Model

The menu model is a very different approach. The image of the menu is, of course, a list of different choices. Each item is separate and distinct from the others. There is no blending here. Every dish retains its own color and flavor. In terms of multicultural realities, the menu image suggests a philosophy that is de facto "separate but equal." We are all one in Christ but we each have our own cultural niche to fill. We have white churches for white folks, black churches for black folks, and congregations and even denominations that cater to certain classes within the complex demographics of our society.

Many in the church growth movement operate on the premise that bringing people together who are like one another is the most effective means of growth and evangelism. Black Christians, white Christians, red Christians, yellow Christians, rich Christians, middle-class Christians, poor Christians; all are true Christians and members of the universal church, the body of Christ. However, if you want *more* Christians, don't try to mix them up all in the same place; let everyone choose her or his favorite dish from the menu.

The most obvious evidence of the menu model of Christianity is the overwhelming cultural segregation of its congregations. Most take shape according to neighborhood patterns of race, ethnicity, and class. The fact that we do not live together and therefore do not worship together means that we also do not think together or sing together. When it comes to aesthetics and our intellectual grasp of the faith, we are undernourished by having only limited choices from the menu. This narrow diet is perpetuated all too often in theological education and continuing theological education. After more than three decades at a seminary, I never cease to be amazed that, despite a varied menu of programs and courses, people almost always choose those representative of their own cultural background.

Some of the greatest African-American preachers of our time have spoken at our seminary's Nelson Trout Lectures in Preaching, but very few white pastors attend. Some of the greatest theologians of various European American traditions have also lectured in other programs, but few African-Americans have come. African-Americans may claim with some justification that they have already had to conform to European American theological traditions. They don't need further exposure to theologies that pay no attention to theirs. However, the bottom line is that we aren't thinking together or singing a new song together.

The Stew Model

The final model, and the one I would commend, is the stew model. The blender model seeks to eliminate differences and the menu model seeks to preserve differences. Neither are adequate to a truly just brand of catholicity. The stew model provides us with an image of diversity in unity. It strikes me as a highly useful portrayal of catholicity for our multicultural world. Our common experience of a stew gets across the message at the basic level just as the blender and menu images did. In a stew all the ingredients retain their own appearance and flavor, but they are together in a common pot so that they flavor each other even as they contribute their own distinctive tastes.

There is no reason why we should not celebrate and learn from the various traditions of that rich global society we call the church. There is no reason why each of these traditions should not retain its own distinctive flavor. There is no reason why the rich variety of Christian traditions should not be together as the church catholic in all its particular manifestations.

There is, of course, nothing new in this idea of diversity in unity. In our previous comments we have already observed that this was the actual situation of the inaugural church at Pentecost. In recent years especially, our hymnbooks have become an amalgam of diverse aesthetic vision and theological emphasis that reflect the history, tradition, and culture out of which the hymns have come. Though they are all translated into a common language, they represent many different spiritual and aesthetic languages of the one Word.

Ecumenical conversations in our time have helped immensely to bring together more and more expressions of the Christian faith from the historically multicultural makeup of the church catholic. Joseph Sittler has noted how Eastern Orthodox participation in the World Council of Churches' Faith and Order talks in the earlier part of the twentieth century helped to open up new vistas for Christology and the doctrine of grace. Western Christianity tended to be focused on the somewhat limited notion of Christ as *savior*, offering the individual salvation from sin. However, Eastern Christianity brought in the idea of Christ as *Pantocrator*, through whom grace extended to all creation and to all the enterprises of humankind. As mentioned earlier, this expansion of the scope of grace enabled Sittler to see the redemptive action of God at work everywhere. Moreover, faith engendered by grace and active in love could be no less expansive in its concerns for justice and the good of the whole creation.[17] Sittler did not cease being a premier Lutheran theologian, but his ability to learn from a tradition born of a faraway culture infused the churches he influenced with new insights that strengthened their grasp on justice.

A key point to be taken from this illustration from the ecumenical dialogues is *participation*. Maximizing opportunities to learn from each other is the means to the end of just preaching. A second key point is *complementarity*. Adopting the insights of Christians from other settings does not mean giving up the integrity of your own tradition.

I had a recent experience that I think illustrates both these points. About a year ago I had the privilege of doing an informal workshop for chaplains and some of the medical staff at Kilimanjaro Christian Medical center in Moshi, Tanzania, East Africa. The topic was current issues in ethics and medicine. The emphasis was on participation and sharing far more than on my doing any teaching. We learned from each other and were mutually enriched. Our discussion of the ethics of death and dying provides a prime illustration. I shared the current discussion in our country over assisted dying and recent refinements in the arguments about different variants of euthanasia. They shared with me the fact that their lack of sophisticated resources to keep people alive under extreme circumstances meant that such issues were of little concern in Tanzania. For them the family's readiness to be and remain with their dying loved one up to the very end was the critical sign of moral health.

From them I learned that they had much to teach us about caring for the dying and affirming their dignity through unflinching companionship. From me they learned something of how Christians need to gear up for the kinds of dilemmas progress will bring to them as well. In fact, some of those dilemmas are already among them in covert form, since so often they

involve conflicts of care and cost. Our dialogue helped surface
that reality. The complementarity of our experiences and our
insights gave everyone a fuller picture of the issues for their
own respective contexts.

However, it must also be emphasized that the notions of
participation and complementarity carry within them the imperative of equality. Robert Simmons is right on target in his
comments:

> There are major differences between African-Americans
> and European Americans. When these or any two dif-
> ferent cultures want to worship together, the ethical
> imperative demands the elimination of any assumption
> of one as superior or inferior. The moral imperative de-
> mands unity, harmony, reconciliation, and wholeness in
> Christ. These imperatives require understanding and ac-
> ceptance of differences that prevail over the priority of
> "comfort," "familiarity," and "sameness."[18]

What Simmons is describing is essentially the principles of
justice that are inherent in the process of genuine dialogue.

To be sure, not all manifestations of culturally conditioned
theology are healthy contributions to Christianity. Some cultural influences have pulled theologies outside the orbit of
authentic Christian teaching. The Gnostic heresy in the early
church is a classic example. The religious influences of the surrounding culture blended with Christianity to create a dualistic
system of thought thoroughly incompatible with biblical and
Christian doctrine. Just dialogue throughout the churches that
constitute the church's presence in history will seek to appreciate diversity but also uphold "catholic" doctrine. Catholicity
also includes faithfulness to the dogmas that have defined the
faith for all ages.

Heresy or false teaching is not the only concern, moreover.
The Christian faith can also be distorted by overemphasis on
one aspect of Christian experience at the expense of others.
Paul Tillich once warned about allowing one element of the
human makeup to dominate others in the practice of the faith.
If we allow emotional experience, intellectual grasp, or moral

pursuit to be the litmus test of authentic faith, we run the risk of distortion. All three dimensions of our humanity need to be engaged in a complementary way for the sort of holistic theology appropriate to the biblical tradition.[19] A gift of dialogue can also be the tempering of distortion through the appreciative but critical exchange of views.

It is necessary to briefly signal these caveats about false teaching and distortion in order to acknowledge that the effects of cultural particularity are not always benign or enriching. However, in the final analysis, our capacities as churches for critical appraisal and separatism seem more highly developed than our hunger for sharing. If our preaching of justice as an integral part of the gospel witness in the world is itself to be just, we will need the kind of open dialogue of mutual regard we have been trying to describe.

In a later chapter we shall have more to say about how the sort of dialogue we are advocating *within* the Christian community in the service of just preaching prepares us for dialogue *outside* that community in the service of preaching justice.

FIVE

ECONOMY

*Thesis: Preaching justice means
exposing the greed in our culture
to the light of the divine economy.*

All along the highway, as you approach this particular city, there
is a long line of industrial-park office buildings noteworthy primarily for a relative uniformity of design. They are all pretty
much straight lines, sharp corners, and flat surfaces without vari-
ation, undulation, or ornamentation. Consequently, one hardly
ever notices these structures individually; they all blend in with
one another. However, on a recent trip, one specific unit in that
parade of functional sameness did capture my attention. It too
was a block of a building, an architecturally sterile though doubtless efficient edifice, with windows that were smoothly aligned
with the surfaces of its no-nonsense red brick. So, clearly, it
wasn't its distinctive appearance that caught my eye.

This particular building had one special feature that set it
apart from all the rest. There, taped to one of the windows
facing the highway was a long sign in bold foot-high letters
that read, HAPPY ANNIVERSARY, JULIE, I LOVE YOU. Suddenly
the sterility of this seemingly "all business" bastion of efficiency
was shattered by something dramatically human and profoundly
inefficient, something quite incongruous or odd to the context.

Though this was a refreshing experience, it was an experience
of seeming incongruity. Often pastors may feel that preaching about humane values of Christian love, compassion for the
needy, and justice for the poor may appear incongruous with
the context of business and economics. If they attempt to be a
"sign in the window" by broaching such a conversation between

Christian faith and economic life, they may feel as though they stick out like a sore thumb; they're not even a momentary and delightful deviation in the landscape.

Philip Wogaman has suggested that the intellectual expertise of the economists and the practical experience of the business leaders intimidate preachers. They feel incompetent. They fear that they really have nothing to contribute to the discussion. They don't see how what they have to say fits into the conversation about economic life.[1]

In a similar fashion, I have written concerning the gap that is often felt and experienced between the church and the world of business. In part this gap is a product of a dualistic outlook we have not entirely shaken off. It is a dualism that operates on the premise that business and economic life belong to a realm completely separate from spiritual life. The dichotomy is then strengthened by stereotypes in which the church looks upon all business as morally suspicious at the core and business looks upon the church as out of touch with the real world.[2]

However, the Bible is replete with concerns about the way that we handle our material wealth. The Bible affirms the goodness of all God's creation and the riches of material plenty, which human beings enjoy as a gift from the creator. It sees these vast treasures of creation and our use of them in the framework of an overall economy of harmonious community with God, each other, and the whole earth. This is why greed is condemned (1 Cor. 5:11; 6:9–10; Eph. 5:3–5; Col. 3:5–6). It undermines that wholistic economy in the interest of selfish aggrandizement. By placing personal material gain ahead of God and God's plan for the good of all, it becomes idolatrous.

There is, then, another message to be drawn from the sign in the office window. By injecting an element of human warmth and love into an environment of strict logic and calculation, the sign alerts us to the fact that all enterprises of business and economic life need to be seen as part of a larger complex of values, which economic life exists to serve. Whatever business was being transacted in that office building, it exists not for its own sake but to serve countless "Julies," their spouses, children, and

communities by providing wealth to sustain life and promote
its manifold goods.

Some of this sort of thinking is evident in what is often referred to as stakeholder theory. In this view, business, especially
large corporations, has a complex of moral obligations to the
needs and interests of its many stakeholders, not just to its stockholders. Stakeholders are all who have a stake in the activities of
the organization. These include employees and their families,
customers, suppliers, subsidiaries, communities, and even nations and the environment, as well as stockholders. Management
of the company needs to take into account all these interests.
Profitability is not the only aim, even though it is a necessary pre-
condition to serving other ends. In short, this is a more wholistic
vision of economic life from the standpoint of business.[3]

Some theorists have gone so far as to say that the idea of corporate social responsibility is outmoded. That concept seems to
suggest that business is separate from society and has an obligation *to* society. Instead, we should think of business as an
integral part of the larger whole of human society with responsibilities both to individuals and to the good of the larger
society. This places economics within the ecology of the larger
human enterprise.[4]

We certainly want to applaud the potential of such theories
to move economic institutions toward a more humane concern
for the needs of all the people. However, one wonders at times
whether or not stakeholder thinking isn't more the province
of the academy and less the practice of business itself. The
rash of downsizings that continues to define much of American
business during our century's final decade certainly left many
stakeholders in the lurch while, more often that not, giving
stockholders an immediate and gratifying gain.

To the extent that we have seen stockholder interest trump
stakeholder well-being, we have one illustration of the inequality that has characterized our society for much of its existence.
This is not even to mention parallel and even more profound
inequities in the global community.

On the eve of the 1960s John Kenneth Galbraith, the celebrated economist, in his famous book *The Affluent Society*, wrote

of the American debate over inequality in wealth. He rehearsed the long-held views of the conservatives that the rich should not be frustrated from accumulating wealth by schemes for income redistribution. However, he went on to say that opposition to this viewpoint faded, along with public concern over inequality, due to the fact that inequality did not worsen and increased production promised more benefits for more people.[5] Now, more than forty years since Galbraith wrote that book, production and affluence are greater than could have been imagined. However, according to the Organization for Economic Cooperation and Development, the United States still has the most unequal distribution of wealth of all advanced industrialized nations.[6]

Preaching justice means examining our greed — the underlying personal and cultural forces of self-serving that help create and exacerbate the disparities of our world so damaging to God's will for community in all creation — in the light of God's universal economy.[7]

Greed is as old as the hills. Moreover, the evils of selfish materialism certainly are and have been a favorite topic for preachers. However, if we are to address greed out of a concern for justice, it will require that we only *begin* with matters of personal vice and virtue. We will need to merge concern for character issues with cultural critique and Christian witness. Finally, we must ask by what practices do we live out our witness on behalf of those who suffer the consequences of greed.

CHARACTER AND CULTURAL CRITIQUE

During the last quarter of the twentieth century the field of Christian ethics has seen a renewal of interest in the subject of character and virtue. Thanks to the work of philosopher Alasdair MacIntyre, theologian Stanley Hauerwas, and others, concern for the formation of character and virtue has been rekindled. Along with that has come an appreciation for the importance of story-formed communities as the seedbed of character.[8] A story-formed community is one whose ethos is shaped by a specific narrative, which has the power to enable a perspective on reality and a moral vision. Within such a com-

munity, virtue and character are shaped by the revelatory power
of the narrative and its moral vision. Certainly the church is
one such community, shaped by the biblical narrative of God's
acts in history, culminating in the gospel of Jesus Christ.

However, there are other stories in other communities that
have a similar impact on how we see the world and the sort
of character appropriate to that vision. Christians live in these
other communities under the influence of their various stories
at the same time that they live in the church and are formed
by its narrative.

According to Professor Roger Betsworth, the Enlightenment
story of progress is the narrative that shaped American culture.
By the nineteenth century, Betsworth claims, it was competing
with the biblical story as the "primary vision of self and world."[9]

The belief in progress spawned by the Enlightenment vision
produced two cultural stories. One had to do with America's
leadership among the nations. The other was the gospel of
success. It was the story that emphasized a belief in every
individual's freedom to make personal progress. As the story
evolved, success became linked to wealth and the wealth of the
successful was directly linked to moral virtue. This was a connection evident in the personal stories of cultural "success icons"
like Benjamin Franklin in the early days and Andrew Carnegie
in more recent times. It was brought home to children through
moralistic stories of diligence and the rewards of success in the
McGuffey *Readers*.[10]

Carnegie is of special interest to us since he brings us closer
to our own time and represents one of the classical stories of
business in the American tradition. As Betsworth points out,
Carnegie was a great believer in social Darwinism. This is certainly evident in his article "The Gospel of Wealth." Having
admitted that competition in business creates great inequalities and places the power and wealth in the hands of a few, he
argues that it is still not too great a price to pay. The law of
competition cannot be evaded.

No substitutes for it have been found; and while the law
may be hard for the individual, it is best for the race

because it insures the survival of the fittest in every department. We accept and welcome, therefore, as conditions to
which we must accommodate ourselves, great inequality
of the environment; the concentration of business, indus-
trial and commercial, in the hands of a few; and the law
of competition between these as being not only beneficial,
but essential to the future progress of the race.[11]

While this sort of argument may seem nothing more than a
relic of a less enlightened past, it has nonetheless begotten an
unbroken heritage of inequalities. It would be hard to convince
those left out of the current round of prosperity or those loyal,
effective, long-term employees who have been escorted from
their job sites to the parking lot that Carnegie-type thinking
has vanished from our ethos.

Betsworth is correct in pointing out that the labor movement, the social gospel movement, and various expressions of
the civil-rights movements have all been effective twentieth-
century challenges to the gospel of wealth. They represent
a communitarian vision of mutual concern for one another.
Yet, he must also acknowledge, despite these corrections, that
"the story of success in America still serves as an interpretive
framework for many persons of the rising middle class."[12]

Carnegie firmly believed that individualism, private property,
the law of the accumulation of wealth, and the law of competition were the highest attainments of human society.[13] These are
lasting elements of an American story that places the rights and
aspirations of the individual or individual enterprises ahead of
the good of the whole. Despite egalitarian movements on behalf of the greater community, the disparities that exist in our
society are tolerated to a considerable degree, I suspect, because
of this individualistic tradition.

Tolerance for inequalities is also abetted by a conviction that
there are virtually limitless opportunities for all who want to
pursue them. As long as there is evidence that that is true, we
can accept disparities in goods as largely a matter of personal
choice and motivation. A sense of urgency on behalf of the
poor is thereby defused to some degree. So, we recall Galbraith's

observation that concern over inequality was dampened in our century by the sense of security, which came with the increase of production in the post-war economy. There is reason to be confident. Greed may not always be attractive but it may not be that detrimental to others. "A rising tide floats all boats."

The story of success, of which Carnegie's story is but one of many chapters, might be called an accessory to greed in both its personal and social manifestations. This powerful story has a profound impact upon our character as a people and a strong influence on the identification of the virtues we admire. Christians and others live in a mix of competing narratives. It is easy for confusion to occur as the stories blend into one another. Influential clergy extolled the likes of Carnegie in his day. In our century the church has aligned itself with socialism and Marxism and is now circling back to a more cautious appreciation for democratic capitalism. Perhaps most church leaders are simply trying to play the hand they've been dealt, looking for justice as best they can amidst the inescapable imperfections of the economic order. If this be the case, as I think it is for many, it is a good time to recover the potential of our own Christian story and stories for the cause of economic justice and the Christian character that must drive it in the church's witness.

CHARACTER AND CHRISTIAN WITNESS

Betsworth concludes his discussion of the stories of success by observing that they have great power but even greater flaws. What is powerful is the promise of personal progress. However, this highly individualistic outlook is also the source of the story's greatest shortcomings. It does not recognize that what we have in life is a gift; it emphasizes only the belief that diligent effort produces each individual's success and the rewards are therefore hers or his solely and alone. It is an account of reality that fails to see that real people face real limits, which they cannot readily overcome. Inequalities are not merely a function of choice and industry. Furthermore, the story of success does not include a sense of the multiple relationships that make up life. It focuses only on the path to personal prosperity. In sum,

The story of success is destructive even to those who succeed and count themselves worthwhile. They no longer
live in human community where persons are encouraged
to discover the resources to love one another. There is in
this story no sense of living together in covenant with the
God who cares for the oppressed and therefore bids us
care for the oppressed.[14]

These remarks bring us back to our opening observations.
The material goods of this world are the gift of God for the
beloved creatures that God wills to live in harmonious community with one another. Economic life needs to be understood
as an instrumental value within the web of human community. Economics exist to serve the full range of human values.
(As a symbol, the sign in the window helps remind us of
that.) Human beings exist to walk with God and love one
another.

Loving one another and bringing economic life under that
rubric in biblical terms seems to imply an ethos of sharing. The
notion of sharing does not point us to a particular economic
philosophy or specific ideology of economic justice. Rather, it
conveys a deep sense of being together in life and in human
community. Apart from positing the essentially relational nature
of human existence, sharing would be a strange concept with
no moral force or rationale. Sharing also suggests that the first
thing we want to say about the goods we possess is not that we
possess them. Private ownership is not precluded in the Bible,
but the sense of having stewardship of God's gifts to us is a
stronger theme.

The biblical story, culminating in the Christ event, and the
stories that give it its accents are the foundations of the sort
of community and character commensurate with an ethos of
sharing.

God is a giving God and, one might say, a sharing God who
freely and lovingly provides for humankind and all creatures. In
both Genesis 1 and 2 God provides the blessings of creation for
human beings to enjoy and to care for, not as their own, but as
a gift and trust from God. All the earth and its goods belong to

God (Exod. 19:5; Deut. 10:14, Ps. 24:1) and we share in these goods out of God's generosity (Ps. 145:15–16).

To Abraham and Sarah God gave the miraculous gift of Isaac, the child of promise, whose birth marked the beginning of a chosen people of Abraham and Sarah's descent (Gen. 21:1–7). The chosen people who would emerge from this covenant promise to Abraham are reminded of the giftedness of their existence in the context of the great *Shema* (Deut. 6:4–9). They have been given the promised land filled with cities and houses they did not build and vineyards and groves they did not plant (Deut. 6:10–11). Continually thereafter, the Israelites are reminded over and over again to share with the stranger in their midst and to care for those in need, for they have been delivered from slavery to a new land out of God's generosity.

James 1:17–18 connects this ancient biblical tradition of God's grace with God's grace in the Christ event.

> Every generous act of giving, with every perfect gift, is from above, coming down from the Father of lights, with whom there is no variation or shadow due to change. In fulfillment of his own purpose he gave us birth by the word of truth, so that we would become a kind of first fruits of his creatures.

It is no surprise, then, that James goes on to excoriate those who favor the rich and disdain the poor and to attack the greed of those who cheat their laborers (5:1–6). All such acts are incommensurate with God's generosity.

Undiminished in power by the burden of familiarity, John 3:16 reminds us that God's sharing is not merely the sharing of goods. God gives of God's own self.

In Philippians 2:4–11 we are called upon to have the mind of Christ who emptied himself of his divinity so that he could share our humanity. He shared our humanity even to the point of death on a cross so that we might share in his abundant life.

God gives freely out of love without reservation or condition. God gives the life-sustaining gifts of sun and rain to both the righteous and unrighteous alike. This is a sign of the perfection of divine love (Matt. 5:45–48). Indeed, Paul tells us, "while we still were sinners Christ died for us" (Rom. 5:8).

The story of the Rich Fool (Luke 12:16–21) is not a condemnation of wealth that comes by hard work and good fortune. The problem of this wealthy farmer was his unwillingness to share. He threw a party simply for himself to rejoice in his own good fortune. He stored his surplus in the bigger barns he built so that in the future, should a slack time come along, not only would he have provisions for himself, but others would be dependent on buying from him. His thought was only for his own security and he was smug about his prospects.

The parable of the Rich Man and Lazarus, which occurs later in Luke's Gospel (16:19–31), is also about the failure to share. Lazarus, the poor beggar, covered with sores, was right under the nose of the rich man. Yet, he received nothing. Of course, in the end we see Lazarus with God while the rich man is in torment. This is a parable of eschatological reversal. In God's coming reign all will find a place at the heavenly banquet and the dramatic disparities symbolized so vividly in the contrast between the excess of the rich man and the squalor and misery of Lazarus will be eradicated.[15]

Word and sacrament go together. Preaching justice as sharing in the face of greed is immediately allied with the theological force and efficacious grace of the Eucharist. The Lord's Supper makes us one community in the body and blood of Christ. It is a community created by a gift. It is a community in which there is enough for all and all share equally and mutually in its benefits. It is a community meal that is a foretaste of the heavenly banquet. When we participate in the sacrament of the Lord's Supper, we not only remember Christ's sacrifice in the past, we anticipate the fullness of his promise for the future. That anticipation does not end in the moments of Eucharistic sharing, however. Rather, our Eucharistic experience calls us into the world to extend that activity of anticipation into the structures of our worldly life together. It is a call to leaven the justice of our society with the ethos of sharing.

PREACHING AND PRAXIS

Justice demands that economic life be integrated into the larger
range of values that constitute the good of the human community. This observation has led us to the realization that greed,
the selfish disregard for the needs of others, is destructive of that
communitarian vision. Signs of that destructive influence are
everywhere in the dramatic inequalities of material well-being
all around us. Cultural traditions and stories like the gospel
of wealth or the story of success have helped to make greed
endemic and systemic. However, the biblical story builds a different sort of character, one that seeks justice through avenues
of sharing that imitate the sharing love of God in Christ.

Every newly arrived preacher knows that the more she or
he becomes involved in the lives of the people and the community, the more effective her or his preaching will become.
Preaching and pastoral practice feed off one another. When we
are working at the crossroad of the Word and the life situation, both are illuminated. Through the involvement of God's
people in the arena of human need, the biblical story comes to
life as it intersects with the continually unfolding stories of our
world experience. Preaching justice and engagement in praxis
go together. I want to suggest three "practices" in the life of the
church that serve to punctuate our proclamation. They constitute some of the avenues of sharing that I referred to in the
previous paragraph.

Stewardship

Remembering that we began this entire discussion with the
conviction that justice is at the core of the church's gospel
proclamation, we pose these questions: Does our theology and
program of stewardship in the congregations and the church
as a whole reflect the full scope of our gospel mission in the
world? Do they articulate and foster the act of being involved
in that broad mission?

For many Christians, if not most, the matter of stewardship is a matter of giving money toward church management
and finances. It is a means to an end, the money required to

sustain the church for its true mission. Even the offerings we make of time and talents tend to be associated with internal churchly activities. This is what Douglas John Hall has referred to as a "truncated version" of stewardship, which is largely *self-supporting* in its priorities.[16] Moreover, if there is a mission in the world for the world, sharing our goods through giving to the congregational budget may still leave us one step removed from actual participation.

A broader view of stewardship would build on our recognition that all things belong to God, and that life itself is a gift. It would further take clues from our divinely given, innate being-in-community. A corollary of both those starting points would then be our responsibility for each other and the goods we receive from a generous God.

Giving money to the congregational budget, church benevolence, and lending a hand with necessary church activities certainly fit this broader view of stewardship. However, in the larger vision, ways in which Christians foster the justice of a more sharing society through political, economic, and social means also count as Christian stewardship. As one example, business leaders who concern themselves with the well-being of the communities in which they operate or share the wealth of their enterprise fairly with their employees should be accounted as engaging in a Christian practice of stewardship. This kind of practice concretely captures the sense of community and mutual responsibility that we have been lifting up. As such, it is a direct participation in the mission, not simply giving to the mission. It is stewardship as a practice of justice.

Community Involvement

Another practice, which goes along with the preaching of justice, is community involvement. A powerful step toward a sharing society is to affirm the value of community by seeking to serve and build the communities in which we live. This takes us out of the orbit of individual, private religion that is oblivious to social concerns and can easily be understood as the spiritual counterpart of material greed.

Community involvement is probably better illustrated than

described. Another sample from Nile Harper's collection of
remarkable urban church stories should serve us well.

St. Pius V Roman Catholic Church and six other Catholic
parishes in the Pilsen area on the West Side of Chicago have
a long history of community involvement. The area has undergone ethnic change and since 1974 has become a predominantly
Spanish-speaking Mexican American neighborhood.

The pastor of St. Pius V, Charles W. Dahm, O.P., saw the
need, first of all, to build community involvement on sound
theological foundations. The people brought with them from
their life in Mexico a defeatist attitude that was ready to accept suffering as good and the status quo as unchangeable. In
contrast, Pastor Dahm preached a theology "which sees in Jesus
an affirmation of human dignity, transformation, and struggle
for justice. Jesus is understood as rejecting inequality between
rich and poor; challenging unjust power; denouncing discrimination against women, foreigners and outcasts. . . . "[17] It was this
kind of preaching and teaching that, blended with a tradition
of community involvement, enabled the leadership to engage
those newly arrived in shaping the future of what was now
becoming their community.

The community organizing involvement of St. Pius and her
sister parishes has undergone various developments of organizational alliance, which is instructive as a model of cooperation but
need not detain us here. What is noteworthy for our immediate
concerns is the manner in which the community involvement
projects serve to build community and address unmet needs and
disparities as an expression of responsible community. Here is
a brief account of the accomplishments of what is now known
as The Resurrection Project (TRP), formed by a merger of the
parishes with a local community development organization:

> The Resurrection Project's accomplishments are many
> and include projects in affordable housing, small business
> development, community education, child care, cultural
> programs, housing for seniors, a shelter for homeless
> women, community block clubs, and the development of
> sufficient political power to obtain needed resources for

the community from city, state, and federal government entities. TRP has generated over $18 million in investment in Pilsen and is currently managing in construction, rental renovation, and facility development.[18]

The Pilsen area churches have learned a great deal from their activities in the community, but one thing seems extremely important. That one thing is the recognition that all must understand that they are driven by their Christian faith and its commitment to justice. The ultimate goal is not simply wresting enough power to create change. The goal is to witness to Christ in caring for the neighbors and to engender a community that lives the values of God's kingdom.[19] The blend of preaching and praxis could hardly be clearer than it is in this situation.

Advocacy

Community involvement, as we have just described it, certainly involves advocacy as well as activism. However, the larger venue of the national and international communities is also an arena of Christian witness for justice.

The issues involved in Christian advocacy for certain public policies and economic proposals are significant, especially when we try to address the larger national and global questions. There is disagreement among Christians — even among those convinced that justice is at the center of our message — over how we engage in advocacy. These questions belong more appropriately to the next chapter. For the present it is enough to make the point that the practice of advocacy is a channel for Christian concern over the sort of gaping inequalities of our corporate life that signal the presence of systemic greed.

There are signals aplenty! We have already mentioned the terrible situation with health care delivery in our country. It bears repeating in this context. That over forty-three million people lack health coverage in the world's richest nation sends up a flare that special interests and the apathy of the privileged are perpetuating this scandal. There is enough food for the world's population and yet thousands starve and countless others lack requisite nutrition for a healthy life. It appears that we have not yet learned the art of distribution. What forces lie behind that fact and where is the leverage for change?

As I write this, the United States is anticipating a budget surplus of over a trillion dollars, but we have yet to pay our dues to the United Nations and some in Congress are talking about cutting what is already a stingy foreign aid commitment. As one columnist put it, "The idea of a generous America, leading where it must, sharing where it can and financing the development banks to help those most in need, has a shrinking constituency."[20]

Denominations, ecumenical councils of churches, and ecumenical church-related organizations like Bread for the World have persons actively engaged in the work of advocacy at all levels of government and in dialogue with large corporations. These people and their publications alert us to the issues and the legislative initiatives involved. The public statements and declarations issued by church bodies and ecumenical councils provide biblical, theological, and ethical guidance on many of these concerns.

The social-ministry organizations of our churches are important allies in the preaching of justice and the practice of advocacy. They deal regularly with the sort of suffering that reveals some of the deficits in our mutual care for one another. They are not only equipped to show us the needs and give us opportunities to share with those in want, but they too are engaged in advocacy. Once again, if we understand and affirm that justice is at the heart of the Christian gospel promise, those in social ministries will be regarded as intimate partners in the basic mission of the church.

Perhaps enough has been said about advocacy to suggest how we get our clues and where we can find both help and colleagues in the task. Now it is time for one last story.

THE GREEDY RAT OF TANZANIA

A group of us sat around the dinner table after the evening meal and, as was our custom, we told stories, everything from church gossip to folk tales. The place was a small rural campus in Tanzania and the story I'm sharing was told by a pastor friend named Peter Kijanga.

It seems there was a farmer whose house was infested with rats. He finally became so bothered by the rats that he set a trap and baited it with a piece of fragrant and delicious meat.

That evening, one of the rats, who was very clever, saw and smelled the meat and wanted it badly. However, being as smart as he was, he also saw that this was a trap. So he called to the other rats. As he expected, one of them blundered into the trap. It snapped shut and killed him. Once the trap was sprung, the clever rat could then safely eat the meat.

Each night the farmer put out the trap with another piece of meat and each night the clever and greedy rat pursued the same strategy. After a time, all his fellow rats were dead. There were no more companions to lure into the trap. However, the farmer continued to put out the trap with a delicious piece of meat as bait.

By now the clever rat had become so greedy for the meat that he couldn't live without it. So each night he backed into the trap and let it take off a bit of his tail so that he could then turn around and eat the meat. Soon he had no tail left. He could no longer escape the trap and still eat the meat. However, because his desire for the meat was so great, he could not resist trying for it yet again. That was the end of him.

The moral of the story, said my friend Peter, is that insatiable greed destroys those around you and, bit by bit, destroys you as well.

SIX

WORLD

*Thesis: Preaching justice is the voice
of the Christian community in dialogue,
seeking the will of God.*

The comedian Jackie Mason has a line that never fails to make
me smile. It goes something like this. "I go into to my doctor's
office and on his wall I see his diploma. I don't want to see his
diploma. I want to see his report card!"

Humorous though it may be, this little commentary on life
turns over a very real concern that applies to many endeavors.
We'd like more details before we proceed, if you please. This
is no less the case for the church as it considers the prospects
of involvement in the causes of justice, which we have said is
the praxis that goes with the proclamation. It is not enough to
simply stand for justice or for the broad themes of justice such
as equality or fairness. We need to know in greater detail what
is involved in the struggle for racial justice or economic justice
or environmental justice or just labor practices or justice in the
workplace.

However, to give the old saying "the devil is in the details" a
new spin, knowing the details has frequently been a source of
consternation and irresolution for the church. In chapter 1 we
charted some of the history of the church's uncertainty in matters of justice. That ambivalence is compounded when we get
into specifics on issues of public policy or the detailed workings
of the economic order. Even Christians who believe that justice
is a Christian duty in some real sense may be reluctant to get
in too deep in these complicated arenas of human activity.

In seeking the truth of justice for our troubled world, we

find ourselves enmeshed in the tangled skein of public-policy options and confounded by the seemingly random and runaway developments of economic life. It is this array of uncertainties and conflictual choices, exacerbated in their confusion by the pluralistic cast of our present world, that has prompted some to suggest that the church has no business getting stuck in that mire. We have no Word of God for the proximate decisions of enforcing justice, it is claimed, and we compromise the real message of the Word and our own authority by pretending that we do.

This contention came out very clearly at the 1998 Lambeth Conference, which brought together the bishops of the worldwide Anglican Communion. One of their most controversial decisions was the passage of a resolution enjoining debt cancellation for the most impoverished countries of the world. In connection with this resolution, the bishops saw a video presentation on the effects of debt and of the policies of the International Monetary Fund and the World Bank on poor nations. While this presentation obviously gained the sympathy of the majority as background to the vote, James Wolfensohn, president of the World Bank, who had been invited to speak, met it with an angry response. He expressed both his disagreement with the position presented in the video and his indignation at being asked to speak in such a context. He was applauded by many.[1]

Mr. Wolfensohn did not disagree with the premise that international debt is a matter of grave concern and diminishes needed services in poor countries. However, he also pointed out other contributing factors that need to be considered, such as corrupt government and the failure of the wealthier nations to sustain development assistance. Furthermore, his criticism of the Conference's understanding and analysis of the World Bank and the International Monetary Fund's role played directly to the fears of those who believe the church is not competent to become involved in such matters and has no special expertise to contribute.[2]

In issues of this kind, one can predict that the division of opinion within the Conference would be mirrored by similar disagreements among outside observers, both Christian and non-Christian. Sympathizers will call for renewed challenges to governments and financial institutions. Skeptics will doubtless contend, as many did after the American Catholic Bishops' pastoral letter *Economic Justice for All*, that the bishops simply don't know what they are talking about, either in terms of the interpretation of the facts or the feasibility of the proposal. Others will be quick to point out that the complexity of issues like international debt is only muddled further by the obvious differences in perspective between bishops from the developing countries and those of the industrialized nations. This was quite evident at Lambeth where, in fact, the developing countries dominated the agenda.

The events of Lambeth and the reaction that followed are simply illustrative, not unique. Whenever church bodies attempt to take a stance on matters of justice that profoundly affect public or economic policy, there is bound to be debate of that sort. Lambeth also provides an illustration of the important point that the cultural, socioeconomic, and geopolitical diversity of a global church sometimes produces a diversity of moral opinion.

The complexity of world issues and the diversity of churchly opinion lead ineluctably to the question of authority.

THE QUESTION OF AUTHORITY

By what authority does the church speak on matters of justice? By what authority, then, do we preach on specific issues of justice, except in the most general of terms?

First of all, we need to speak of authority in terms of authorization. "Who put you in charge?" we say to persons who try to take over when they have no right to do so. "Who gave you the right to make judgments about this?" We expect that there will be some orderly mechanism by which people are given authority to render judgments and make decisions.

What is the authorization we have as church to take a public position on issues of justice? The answer is, "It is our calling to do so." As we tried to establish in chapter 1, the church's vocation and its proclamation include addressing and pursuing the cause of justice.

However, as intimated in that discussion and now in this one, there will certainly be gainsayers. They may try to make the case that for issues of justice and keeping the peace God has provided government (Rom. 13:1–7). As for the need to regulate scientific activities or evaluate and review the relative justice of economic policies, we have no biblical direction at all, according to this view.

This is true in part, but not adequate as a whole. Certainly, God has ordained government for the common good and the Bible is hardly a manual for public-policy development. Nonetheless, as we also pointed out in that first chapter, the church has a call to witness to the promise of God's future in the revelation of the Christ. That future, we said, will be marked by values of life, peace, justice, and wholeness. The church witnesses to its faith and hope in the promise of these ultimate values when it seeks their realization in penultimate forms. In the circumstances of life where these values are at stake, the church cannot be silent within its own precincts or within the precincts of government in which its people are participants. If the Christian faith were simply a personal and private affair, it would be different. However, that is not the case. God is the creator and redeemer of the whole world.

Fair enough. We are authorized by a call that involves witness to God's promise and concern for justice. However, authorization is only one aspect of authority. What about the authority that comes with the assurance or confidence in what one is doing? People gain authority among us when they know what they are doing and are convincing and assured. Being officially appointed or elected and thereby authorized isn't enough.

We normally think of authoritative people as the sort of persons who feel sure of themselves when they state their beliefs. They know what they are talking about. They have credibility. People often expect the same kind of certainty in connection with moral judgments. To be sure, we have much to go by in this regard. As we have just reminded ourselves, the Bible provides us with a vision of the values we seek. The norms of Scripture

and their development in the traditions of the church teach us
a great deal about the kind of conduct that serves those values. We know about Christian love and we know that it seeks
justice through mercy. The Bible lifts up the needs of the poor
and oppressed as being at the top of God's agenda. It does not
require sophisticated scholarship to see this in clear focus.

The real problem for establishing our authority in terms of
credibility is in the interpretation of how our Christian principles and values apply to specific circumstances. It is one thing
to state that the growing gap between the poor and wealthy
is evidence of systemic economic injustice. It is another thing
to argue about the particular trade policies our country should
adopt as a corrective measure. It is one thing to argue that justice
requires uniform international standards of safety in pharma-
ceuticals. It is another thing to determine whether a drug not
meeting standards in one country is still safe enough for use
in another setting where it is desperately needed and the only
alternative at present. It is one thing to argue that there should
be fair distribution of wealth throughout the workforce. It may
not be as easy to maintain that therefore labor has the right
to organize even in nonprofit settings, like long-term care fa-
cilities, where margins are low and clients are dependent on
uninterrupted care.

In situations like these and in many others that come readily
to mind, we face both our limits and our limitations.

The limits we live with are those that come with being finite
creatures. Theologically speaking we are *image* of God, not all-
knowing, self-sufficient gods. We have limitations in that we
are sinful people in a sinful world, persons fraught with the
imperfections of our fallen state in an imperfect world.

Our inability to fully understand the facts we deal with in
complex situations or see clearly the alternatives and the possible
outcomes is simply a reality. Like Jackie Mason, we'd like to see
the report card. That is, we'd like to know enough to be sure
about our choices. But this will not always be the case.

The limitation of our flawed motives sometimes asserts itself
in complex circumstances where the stakeholders involved have
conflicting claims. Our defensive urge toward self-justification

may obscure other viewpoints on the problem that we need to see and hear. The prejudices we bring to the situation may distort our perceptions of some salient facts. In any major debate over a complex issue it's a cinch that no one of the parties involved will have all the facts or all the insights.

Even when we try our best to check the distorting effects of prejudicial motives and do our best to overcome the limits of knowledge involved, the world we live in often forces us to make unfortunate compromises and even tragic choices. We preach justice but find that there is no perfectly just solution given the alternatives we have.

In the final analysis, however, our assurance, our confidence, and our courage to face the challenges of ethical decision-making come not from certainty about being right, but from the assurance of God's promise. We are God's people, accepted, forgiven, set apart. Though our efforts to love and serve the neighbor and the world are flawed, God accepts those efforts as good and sends us out again and again.

Though our authority and confidence reside in the call and the promise we have as the people of God, when we lift our voice on behalf of justice, we must do so responsibly. Our methods of seeking the right understanding of what justice demands in a complex world must be both credible and consistent with the impulse of our faith.

AUTHORITY AND DIALOGUE

Despite his negative reaction to the video on the role of the World Bank and the International Monetary Fund in the matter of debt, Mr. Wolfensohn was not opposed to the idea of the church being involved in partnership with others to address the problem of poverty. One of his comments provides a good introduction to this section of our discussion. "The reason that I have come to admire the Archbishop of Canterbury to such an enormous extent is that he has shown to me an openness to say, 'We're both fighting poverty. Let's see what we can do together.'"[3]

The Archbishop's collegial proposal points us directly to the idea of dialogue. Finding our way to the best possible response to complicated and conflictual issues of justice requires a process of dialogue. Dialogue involves serious engagement with one's dialogue partners. It involves a readiness to be attentive to the concerns, knowledge, and insights of those partners. Dialogue requires that we respect what our partners have to offer and be open to new discoveries. Dialogue also enables us to be as clear about our own beliefs as we allow others to be. If we are dogmatic in our approach, there is no dialogue. If others are similarly rigid and closed to our faith-based contributions, there is no dialogue. If there is no dialogue, we are locked into the narrow confines of our limits and limitations. If there is dialogue, we are all on a path to greater discovery about the demands of justice in our world.

There is both grace and justice in dialogue. For people of faith the element of grace is in the assurance that we are free in the gospel to venture forth into the uncharted waters of this kind of interaction. There is also grace in the ministry of the Spirit along the way to aid us in dealing with both our limits and our limitations. There is justice in dialogue's demand for mutual respect and honesty.

Though it is probably an oversimplification, we can speak of two interlocking spheres of dialogue. The one is with the world around us and the other is within the community of faith.

Dialogue with the world around us on matters of justice happens in a myriad of ways. It happens through individual Christians engaged in their vocations as citizens and as participants in economic life. It happens through public discourse through a variety of media as positions espoused by the church or questions raised by the church draw response. Dialogue happens in educational settings. It happens through representatives of Christian communities interacting with government at all levels and with corporate boards or industry representatives. It happens through the advocacy work of nongovernmental organizations of Christian constituency and the social ministry organizations of the church discussed in the previous chapter. Sometimes special events in the life of the church or the society provide opportunities. An Earth Summit, anniversary of the U.N. Declaration of Human Rights, or similar global or local observance and gathering are one kind of example. Papal visits, ecumenical assemblies and councils, and anniversaries like those connected with the Reformation are another kind of example.

Wherever and however dialogue is generated between the church and society on issues of justice, the church will want to seek the truth, subject its own views to the analysis of others, and weigh the insights dialogue partners can contribute. It seeks the truth in terms of the best possible knowledge and understanding of the facts. It seeks the truth of its own motives and the motives of others. The church is open to the critique of those it has critiqued. It is open not only to a better understanding of what is just, but also to a better understanding of what is possible and how to go about it.

Christians in dialogue with the world may also discover in new ways the proximate character of their own insight as the world fills the forms of love with its demands for justice. New ethical insights stemming from the voices of those who suffer and further informed by the social and political sciences have reversed the prejudicial attitudes and practices of the church in the past and beamed light on its blind spots in areas such as race, access for persons with disabilities, and the role and rights of women.

We have been given the grace to receive such revelations with repentance and gratitude. Our confidence is not in our unbroken record of being right, but in God's unbroken promise.

In our pluralistic world of many diverse viewpoints shaped by a variety of cultural and religious forces, there is a real danger that justice will suffer from ethical relativity. Christian participation in dialogue does not mean compromise of our principles and values for the lowest common denominator. Rather, it means pursuing a path to the discovery of common convictions in the midst of diverse traditions, all in the service of justice.

However, if Christian participation in worldly dialogues is going to go forward with integrity, dialogue within the community must be a constant companion. Preaching justice is not only the church in dialogue with the world seeking the will of God. Preaching justice is also the church in dialogue with itself seeking the will of God. In his article "Preaching as the Church's Language," Richard Lischer observes, "[The] church exists for the world, but it renews its identity when it gathers for worship. It speaks in the world, but it learns its 'distinctive talk' when its members come together around word and sacrament."[4] That is why preaching justice is so important to doing justice. Preaching is integral to Word and Sacrament ministry and Word and Sacrament ministry is what shapes us as a people. The grace and community that are ours provide the wherewithal and the context for the dialogue we need among ourselves to equip us for our witness in dialogue with the world. With the sharing of our manifold talents and experiences, we profit from an enlarged capacity for discerning the will of God as God's word intersects with our world.

At this point in our discussion of preaching justice in dialogue with the world, we are perhaps best served by a brief example.

JUSTICE FOR THE WHOLE WORLD

In today's world we have become permanently aware of the fact that preaching justice means justice for the whole world, not just the human community. The environmentalism that has emerged during the last half-century has forced the church into a dialogue concerning the care of the earth. What the church has learned from that dialogue illustrates the possibility of new discoveries and a chastened reconsideration of one's own views.

As most everyone is aware, the history of Christian thought has not always been environmentally friendly by today's standards. Rather, as Paul Santmire has shown in his book *The Travail of Nature*, Christian theology has been ambiguous about its concern with the world of nature. Its attention has been on human well-being and destiny or on the spiritual as opposed to the material. Some have accused Christianity of promoting an anthropology that gives humanity the God-given right to exploit the earth. Even though this is not quite true, the neglect of nature and the focus on human need may have led people to that conclusion.[5]

In addition to the insights and appropriate admonitions the church gains from its participation in the public dialogue on environmental justice, it receives essential information for its own commitments to justice for the earth. Scientific data is obviously critical. Knowledge of economic factors that impinge on our assessment of what we can and ought to do is another important requirement for responsible decision-making. Political realities are also something we always deal with in setting public policy for environmental justice. Political savvy comes out of dialogue with multiple stakeholders. However, knowledge or even "facts" do not resolve questions of our moral obligation to justice. Sometimes they make ethical decision-making even more difficult because the facts themselves are disputed and knowledge involves interpretation. An example helps to make the point.

Not long ago our local newspaper ran an opposing-views forum on the editorial page. The subject was the much debated issue of global warming. One article was entitled, "Drought, Hurricanes Prove There's a Big Change in the Weather." To support his concern that global warming is a real threat, one author appealed to two public statements by large groups of distinguished scientists. These scientists pointed to evidence that global warming is real and its impact can be documented. The author added that simple observation of recent dramatic weather developments, in addition to scientific testimony, should convince us that it is time to do something definitive about the problem.

By contrast, the other article argued that Vice President Gore's campaign against the threat of human-caused global warming lacks sufficient basis in reality. Here too the appeal was to evidence offered by major scientists engaged in the study of the matter. However, in this account the contention was that the evidence is far from conclusive as to what forces affect climate changes.[6]

Examples of this kind of debate over environmental issues

are easy to multiply. They warn us of the sort of minefield we
must traverse if we are to enter this public discussion on behalf of justice for the earth. However, these disputes also lift
up the necessity of having convictions about human responsibility for nature that are more deeply rooted than those we
can derive from scientific studies alone. In the absence of a
firm moral grounding for the care of the earth, our behavior
and our policies will be continually subjected to every shifting
wind of scientific opinion. It will be an endless round of point-
counterpoint. Therefore, what the faith community brings to
the dialogue is of great importance to a secular world whose
reliance on reason has left it in a quandary.

Creation

If our concern for the environment is to be rooted in something
more than speculation on scientific reports, we need to find a
way to establish the intrinsic value of all of nature. If nature
remains in our minds an aggregate of resources that are simply
of instrumental value, something we use, then it is hard to think
of what our responsibility toward nature is beyond the prudent
steps we take in our own best interests. It will merely be a matter
of good management, challenging as that may be. We conserve
so we can continue to consume and we preserve what's left of
undeveloped nature so we can continue to enjoy it.

    Our biblical faith invites us to consider that there is more to
it than that. To begin with, we affirm that God is the creator of
all things and that God has looked upon *all things* in creation
as "very good." The psalmist echoes the creation account in
lyrical fashion. "The earth is the Lord's and all that is in it,
the world, and those who live in it; for he has founded it on
the seas, and established it on the rivers" (Ps. 24:1–2). God
loves that good creation and continues to bless it and renew
its vitality. God's creating is continuous: "When you send forth
your spirit, they are created; and you renew the face of the
ground" (Ps. 104:30). Creation is God's handiwork and, because
God values it and loves it, it possesses intrinsic value deserving
of our respect.

Thus we hear that Yahweh knows the birds of the air (Ps. 50:11), that [Yahweh] calls the stars by name (Isa. 40:26), that both animals and humans are in [Yahweh's] care (Ps. 36:6), and that [Yahweh] feeds them all.[7]

The intrinsic value creation possesses in God's care for the earth is underscored by the responsibility God has given us. Genesis 1:28 speaks of humanity's "dominion" over all other living things. This same assertion occurs in Psalm 8:6–8. Much mischief has been made over this notion of "dominion" as the key to why biblical religions have allegedly sanctioned the exploitation of the earth. However, scholars have pointed out that this relatively rare biblical term has never had a major role to play in Jewish or Christian thought.[8] The more important concept in that narrative of humanity's creation is the concept of the "image of God."

Humanity's creation in the divine image is what sets the terms for any meanings we can assign to the idea of dominion. The narrative makes clear, first of all, that we are *image* of God, not gods unto ourselves. Our being emanates from and derives its identity from our dependent relationship to God. The metaphorical force of "image" is heightened when we delve into the meaning of the underlying Hebrew word *tselem. Tselem* means image in the sense of a hewn or carved copy of something else. When kings who conquered territories in the ancient Near East left for home, they often left their *tselem,* statues of themselves, behind to represent their sovereignty and remind the conquered peoples of who their ruler was. In an analogous way, as God's *tselem* in the midst of the good creation, we are called upon to care for it as God does. This is true representation.[9] "Caring" is the operative word when it comes to the creation, not "exploitation" or even the more subdued word "use."

When we love God, we love the things God loves in accordance with the way God loves them. This means obviously that we love one another as God loves us, but it also means we love the creation as God loves it. Matthew 6:26–30 is another reminder that God cares for the birds of the air and sustains the lilies of the field in all their beauty, but also that we hold a special place of priority in God's love. How we understand that fact and what that means for our responsibility to love nature as God does and care for it as God's representatives is a subject to which we will return. For now it is sufficient to take the clues that our biblical theology of creation gives us for establishing the intrinsic value of nature as a premise for environmental justice.

Cross and Resurrection

The Christian theology of the cross holds a mirror up to the brokenness of our world. It reflects the truth of our broken relations with God and with each other. It is also a sign under which we can better understand the ambiguity of nature itself.

Certainly the theology of the cross exposes our self-centered estrangement from God and one another and the virtual enmity that ensues. It is that selfishness which leads us into lovelessness and injustice. In the cross we see sin for what it is, a cause of incalculable suffering that comes from our having stepped outside the limits of being image of God and choosing instead to be gods for ourselves. In terms of the environment, the effect of this casting aside of created limits was captured neatly by Reinhold Niebuhr years ago. As James Nash put it, he was ahead of his time in his recognition of ecological sin though not in his use of sexually exclusive language(!).

> Man's sense of dependence upon nature and his reverent gratitude toward the miracle of nature's perennial abundance is destroyed by his arrogant sense of independence and his greedy effort to overcome the insecurity of nature's rhythms and seasons by garnering her stores with excessive zeal and beyond natural requirements. Greed is in short the expression of man's inordinate ambition to hide his insecurity in nature.[10]

What greed does, of course, is not only to exploit nature but also to create intractable injustice and poverty. Injustice toward the earth by disdain for the limits of our call to care is a thread so tightly intertwined with injustice toward each other that the two cannot be pulled apart.

When Jesus appeared as the incarnate one, the Son of God, the Word made flesh, it was a statement of God's ongoing affirmation of the fleshly, material world of creation. When Jesus was lifted up on the cross it was a sign of how intimately God is involved in that affirmation, enough to enter the sufferings of our apostasy in order to make of us a new creation.

The intensity of God's determined identification with created humanity, revealed in the cross, points us to God's deep involvement with the whole of creation, which like humankind has been in "bondage to decay" and has been "groaning in labor pains" (Rom. 8:21–22). Nature as we experience it is an ambiguous blend of good and evil, beauty and ugliness, vitality and decay, a source of joy and great pain.

Larry Rasmussen talks about justice for the creation in terms of harmonious order. However, the void and darkness of the chaos over which the Spirit hovered (Gen. 1:2) keeps intruding on that harmony. There is a "pervasive disorder... deeply embedded within the creation," encompassing both human disasters and natural disasters.[11] As Paul connects the "groaning" of creation with the groaning of a fallen humanity, so we may readily connect the cross with the redemption of both humanity and the whole of creation. God's creating work and God's redeeming work are also like two threads so tightly intertwined that they can't be pulled apart.

The cross helps us to understand that God is with us in the brokenness and ambiguity of all we experience in our lives and in our world. Sin is real, but the promise of God's compassion in the cross is real too. We bring both realities to the dialogue, the story of our arrogance and the story of our hope. We neither romanticize nature nor overestimate humanity. We never underestimate the power and depth of God's love.

Thus, it is not surprising that the promise of the resurrection for God's coming future is as comprehensive as the creation itself and as extensive as God's identification with the sufferings of the whole creation. The resurrection is a victory for the flesh and a hope for the entire material world, the sure promise of

a new creation. The Bible is clear on this, as we affirmed in
chapter 1.

The promise of the resurrection for the new creation in the
reign of God calls us in our quest for environmental justice and
justice in general to an ethic of anticipation. We seek to care
for the earth in anticipation of its final emancipation. We strive
in hope as a witness to our firm belief that in God's final future
the chaos of our disorder will be fully overcome. We are drawn
as by a magnet toward the promised future. Others in the public
dialogue may not share such visions and hopes. However, we
bring a hope and energy generated by God's promise that also
has a magnetic pull on those who come close to it.

Many of these thoughts that I am trying to articulate in the
language of theological discourse came together for me in the
concreteness of a simple but extraordinary experience. I'd like
to take a break from our constructive reflections for a moment
and share it with you.

Interlude

We had been sitting for two days of heavy conversation. The
conference was at a lovely state park called Deer Creek and I was
getting eager to get outside in it and away from meeting rooms.
So, on the third day, at early dawn, I set out for a bike ride.

In search of maximum solitude in which to enjoy the feel of
my muscles in motion and the exquisite quiet of a fresh and
beautiful new day, I turned onto a less traveled side road, which
wound through trees and tall grasses. The tires hummed softly
and I rode contentedly at a comfortable pace.

Suddenly, there they were, right in front of me. Six rabbits
had left the cover of the brush to eat a breakfast of dew-covered
clover on the grassy berm of that remote road. I fully expected
them to scatter at the sound and sight of me. But they did not.
They simply looked up at me, almost as if they expected me
and did not think it at all strange that I should be there. They
went right on chewing the sweet clover, tacitly inviting me, it
seemed, to join them if I wished.

At another time I might have menaced them and chased one
of their kind for eating the tender shoots in my garden. At

another time I might have accidentally struck one of them with
my car. At another time someone who looked like me, a two-
legged creature, might have gone after them with a gun. But
not this time. This time there was no need to run and no need
to chase. It was simply a matter of sharing the beauty of the
morning together, the rabbits and me.

Ours is a world in which there is much running and chas-
ing. It is a world of violence, violence against one another
and violence against other creatures and against the land itself.
However, the encounter with the Deer Creek rabbits evoked a
very different vision of the world. It is one that comes to us
from the prophet Isaiah in these familiar and stirring words:

> The wolf shall live with the lamb,
> the leopard shall lie down with the kid,
> the calf and the lion and the fatling together,
> and a little child shall lead them.
> The cow and the bear shall graze,
> their young shall lie down together;
> and the lion shall eat straw like the ox.
> . . . .
> They will not hurt or destroy
> on all my holy mountain;
> for the earth will be full of the knowledge of the Lord
> as the waters cover the sea.
>
> (Isa. 11:6–7, 9)

This lyrical anticipation of God's promised future is a vision
of hope begotten of God's determination to end the disorder
of sin that has infected all of creation. God has made peace
with us and promised a peaceable kingdom. It is a promise of
peace that calls us to be peacemakers in a world of conflict and
to care for the earth as we care for each other.

These were the thoughts evoked on that third day at early
dawn when I set out to ride. For it was then that I met the
Deer Creek rabbits, who saw their enemy coming, but let him
share the delight of their breakfast moment nonetheless. I was
reminded that on another third day at early dawn, long ago,
Jesus destroyed sin and death and revealed that, in the end,

harmony will pervade the whole creation and the world will teem with everlasting life.

Thus it is that God gives us moments of grace in the present to sustain our faith and hope in the promised future.

Models of Responsibility

Our theology of creation, cross, and resurrection are the foundation stones of the environmental ethic we bring to dialogue with the world. These fundamental elements of our faith lead us to see the inherent value of all creation, to face the reality of our sins against the earth. They are also means of grace that continually renew our hope and energy for the task of environmental justice. Yet, there is more to be said. We need greater clarity about the nature of humanity's relation to nature if we are to offer greater precision in our account of human responsibility for environmental justice.

Larry Rasmussen has offered a number of models by which to characterize humanity's relationship with God and the creation. They provide Christians with some helpful clues. There are three that I think are particularly useful in the present context.[12]

The model of the Steward has a good deal of resonance for many Christians. It replaces the theme of dominion with one of responsibility and care. It calls upon us to cherish all of God's works in nature, to love them as God loves them. Though not all versions of the steward model include this provision, it certainly does allow for asserting the obligation to respect the innate value of the earth and all that is in it. At the same time, the notion of the steward still retains the special place of humankind as image of God in the scheme of creation. This is still a bit too anthropocentric for some tastes, Rasmussen notes, but it is a far more congenial view of human agency than one of domination or even exploitation.

In the Partner model the stress is on the interdependence, interconnectedness, and mutuality of all creatures. Here the intrinsic value of all and the consequent moral obligation to all become a prominent feature. Human beings have special capacities and unique moral obligations, but not as the center of all

things. Rather, ours is an obligation to refrain from disrupting
the ecology of the creation and to embrace a simple lifestyle in
the pursuit of that aim.

The Sacrament/Priest model is a panentheistic approach.
Panentheism posits the presence of God in, with, and under
all of nature. The whole of our world possesses sanctity because God is present in the world. But the world is not God
(that's pantheism), and the world is not in itself worshipped.
The world is *of* God. As we do with the sacraments, we re-
spond in awe and respect. Our sense of the gracious, creative
presence of the infinite God in finite nature evokes an ethic of
care, respect, advocacy — an attitude of species humility rather
than arrogant dominance or oversight. Through this ethic and
by this attitude, we serve a kind of priestly function of me-
diating and communicating the dimension of the holy that is
present in the ordinary.

It strikes me that these three models connect with one another at several points to provide us with a picture of the kind
of character that should underlie Christian concern for environmental justice. It is a character of humility before God the
creator and respect and care for the works of creation.

Our basic theology of creation, cross, and resurrection establish the value of the creation as foundational to environmental
justice. The models of responsibility emanating from Christian
tradition give substance to the character required. Now there is
one final step. We need to identify the norms that define our respect for the essential value of the earth and that give direction
to our responsibility.

NORMS FOR EARTH JUSTICE

In 1989 the Presbyterian Church (U.S.A.) published *Keeping
and Healing the Creation*, a small resource book prepared by their
Eco-Justice Task Force. In this discussion the task force lifts up
four norms that continue to be representative of much of the
discourse on eco-justice, both inside and outside the Christian
community.[13]

Sustainability

"As a norm of human behavior, sustainability requires that we relate to the realm of nature in ways that respect its integrity, so that natural systems continue to function properly, the earth's beauty and fruitfulness may be maintained and kept sufficient for human sustenance, and life may continue also for the non-human species."[14] This norm places the burden of proof on all human enterprises that threaten the integrity of nature and its sustainability. It is a norm that is future oriented, reminding us that our responsibilities extend beyond our own immediate gratification. Under the rubric of sustainability, economic justice and environmental justice coalesce. Yet the effective co-ordination of the two is, as the task force recognizes, always a work in progress, an ongoing constructive dialogue. Perhaps, more than any of the others to follow, this norm highlights the intrinsic value of the whole creation.

Participation

Participation is a norm of justice that lifts up distributive justice in general within the context of eco-justice in particular. God's gifts of the creation are for everyone. If some are left out of adequate access to nature's bounty, something is awry. Economic arrangements should enable participation. Caring for the integrity and sustainability of the earth is in the service of participation.

Sufficiency

A companion to participation, sufficiency is a norm that underscores everyone's right to have enough for his or her basic needs. However, in addition, it calls upon all of us to recognize that "enough" also means "not too much." There are limits within which we need to operate so that all may have a sufficiency of the earth's resources. In other words, this is a principle that points in the direction of developing a sharing society as foundational to justice.

Solidarity

Solidarity reminds us of the essentially communitarian character of eco-justice. First of all, it means linking arms with others who share our concern for the well-being of the planet. Adequate strategies of economic policy and public policy in service of the environment require collaboration among many parties. We need a smaller community of like-mindedness for mutual support in the long battle. We need the larger community of collaboration and coalitions, of public dialogue, to keep our policies on track. We were created for community with God, one another, and the earth. This norm lifts up those communal dimensions of our creation theology.

Second, solidarity means standing together with those poor who are most profoundly affected by the economic and ecological imbalances of our world. Standing with them is part and parcel of the empathic nature of Christian love in its quest for justice. However, solidarity with the most affected is also the venue for a deeper understanding of what our adherence to the other norms for eco-justice means in more concrete terms.

This thumbnail sketch of some of the theological resources for environmental justice gives us at least a glimpse of what we bring to the complex dialogue this concern entails. I make no pretense to an adequate treatment of environmental ethics. We have simply used this snapshot as one example of a justice concern that brings the church into dialogue with the world. The process of dialogue strengthens the witness of our preaching. Attention to the theological and ethical resources we bring to the table gives both content and depth to our preaching.

SEVEN

GRACE

*Thesis: Preaching justice means
living by God's promise.*

Do not let your hearts be troubled. Believe in God, believe
also in me. In my Father's house there are many dwelling
places. If it were not so, would I have told you that I go
to prepare a place for you? And if I go and prepare a place
for you, I will come again and will take you to myself, so
that where I am, there you may be also.... Very truly, I
tell you, the one who believes in me will also do the works
that I do and, in fact, will do greater works than these,
because I am going to the Father. I will do whatever you
ask in my name, so that the Father may be glorified in the
Son. If in my name you ask me for anything, I will do it.
(John 14:1–3, 12–14)

It had been a seemingly endless drive. Fatigue had settled
into every one of us. It was an oft-told tale of a family trip: a
cranky crew desperately looking for a motel with a vacancy. The
excitement and anticipation that marked the day's beginning
had dissipated hours ago. Finally we found a place with a room
to rent. Sleep and refreshment was in sight as we stepped aboard
the elevator. It was then that I noticed one our little daughters.
Angie had become wide-eyed. She was revived by excitement
over being in this large hotel which to her child's eyes appeared
quite glamorous and wonderful. Suddenly, she blurted out, "Is
heaven like a Holiday Inn?" We laughed, as you might expect.
However, I later remembered the passage from John 14, "In my
Father's house there are many dwelling places."

Perhaps there is a bit more depth to the illustrative possibilities of this incident than just a cute, unwitting connection
between heaven and hotels. There is a kind of analogy to be
found in that past episode that prompts some further thought
about John 14 and about our life of discipleship. The family's
journey had been tiring and long. Enthusiasm had given way to
desperation and an intense desire to be done with the trip. The
promise of a welcoming place of rest for weary travelers would
seem like heaven indeed, just as the arduous trip would seem to
resemble at times the journey of following Christ.

"Do not let your hearts be troubled. Trust me. Your future
with God is assured and, in the meantime, ask anything in my
name and I will be there for you." That's the nub of Jesus'
promise and a wonderful promise it is. It is a promise for those
of us who are on the road and finding the going tough. In other
words, it is a good and fitting promise for any time; believing
in God and in the triumph of God's goodness and justice is
always under challenge.

The impenetrable mystery of evil in random killings driven
by demons of hate and insanity within faceless killers pushes
the envelope of faith to its outermost edge. Tribal slaughter in
Rwanda, the Balkans, East Timor, and elsewhere have erupted
in the past decade, which was supposed to see the dawn of a new
world order of peace, justice, freedom, and prosperity. Instead it
evokes a dispiriting horror. And these are only the high-profile
stories of the present moment. At the same time that we lament
these dreadful events, thousands are dying a quiet, invisible death
from starvation and lack of medical attention, not because food
or medical care is in short supply, but because we lack the political will to distribute it justly. In our own prosperous country over
forty-three million are now without health care. Needy children
literally get lost in the foster-care system or abused in the ju-
venile detention system because of a combination of ignorance
and sloth, not to mention occasional cruelty.

Are we ever going to gain on the problem of injustice in its
manifold forms? It's enough to make you want to quit. How can
we preach justice without sounding out of touch with reality?
Will not our words seem only vacuous to those hardened in their

cynicism and stirring only to the naïve? Maybe those folks we talked about earlier who said the church should concentrate on personal salvation and not social justice had something after all? They are still around and still willing to give you the same message or to simply be quietly unresponsive to the proclamation of justice.

"Do not let your hearts be troubled. Trust me. You will have what you need to do the works you are called in me to do." That is what we have as Christian people, a promise — a promise for the time in which we live, and that time is "for the time being." That time is the "in-between time." It is a promise for the present rooted in a future that is not yet.

THE GIFT OF MOURNING

One of the gifts we receive for the works Jesus promised us we would do is the gift of mourning. At first it seems that this is an ambiguous gift to say the least and often in our life journey it feels like a burdensome gift. However, in truth, it is an enabling gift of grace. When Jesus said, "Blessed are those who mourn, for they will be comforted" (Matt. 5:4), he both described life in the in-between time and gave us a promise not unlike the one recorded in John 14. He was announcing a new capacity for the vocation of those who live in him and adding to that a promise to give the strength needed to fulfill that calling.[1]

The capacity to mourn is the ability to feel pain and empathy when confronted with loss and suffering. It is the gift of being able to enter into that suffering with one's own heart. It is the gift of being one with Jesus, who grieved over Lazarus and who had compassion on the hungry crowd. To be able to mourn is the grace to be one with Jesus who cared for lepers, whom no one would go near, and who was moved by the woman who strained her way through the pressing crowd with simply the hope of touching the hem of his garment. The gift is to be one with Jesus, who wept over his people, Israel, and who entered so deeply into our suffering that he endured our pain, rejection, injustice, betrayal, cruelty, brutality, humiliation, and death.

To be one with Christ is to be given the gracious gift of

mourning, of feeling, of caring, of grieving, of solidarity with those who suffer. It is the virtue of love's character that energizes the norm of solidarity that we spoke of in the last chapter. Were we untouched by the grace of Christ, we would lack his capacity to give of himself and open up his life to ours. However, by grace we are being transformed in his image, Paul tells us (2 Cor. 3:18). That is to say, we are being turned from selfish disregard for God and one another toward love for God and one another. For the Christian, total self-centeredness and emotional isolation is a "luxury" outside our possibilities. We can neither turn our backs upon the victims of injustice who are among us, as though they were strangers, nor can we fail to feel the pain of those unjustly treated who are strangers far away from us.

In his widely appreciated book *The Wounded Healer,* the late Henri Nouwen wrote of how the pastor can make the experience of his or her own wounds a source of healing in ministry. It is not a matter of commiseration, a kind of "misery loves company" approach to ministry. Rather, said Nouwen, "Making one's own wounds a source of healing, therefore, does not call for a sharing of superficial personal pains but for a constant willingness to see one's own pain and suffering as rising from the depth of the human condition, which all [persons] share."[2]

The grace of solidarity with the suffering that we have been trying to get at in our talk about mourning is the grace to recognize the pain of the world's injustice as emanating from a common reality. Neither the source nor the effects of injustice are alien to us; they are elements of a shared condition in which we are implicated by virtue of our humanity. The dispiriting frustrations or even fears experienced in preaching justice are not imposed upon us from the outside, as by a heartless public or a callused church. Even though we feel like victims of disdain for justice, in the greater depth of our shared human condition we are also the perpetrators. Once we realize this, we can begin the healing by preaching justice out of the depths of the gospel, which alone can speak to the depths of our wounded condition. Knowing that we are always together in sin and in Christian hope, we shall never be tempted to launch the church's proclamation of justice from the prideful platform of moralism.

This particular application of Nouwen's basic insight is not
simply meant for the preacher who may feel at times like Elijah
("I alone am left, and they are seeking my life," 1 Kings 19:10).
It is for the whole church in its corporate mission for justice.
In its marriage of proclamation and praxis, the church is drawn
ever deeper into the depths of its own identity with the whole
of humankind and finds there the utter truth of the gospel. In
this way it is continually renewed for mission.

Blessed are those who mourn, for they shall be wounded
healers. And they shall be comforted.

PROLEPTIC MOMENTS

The promise of "comforting" attending the beatitude is not one
simply of being soothed or made to feel better; it is a promise
that we shall be strengthened for the call to solidarity. It is much
like the promise Jesus gives the disciples in John 14 that they
will be equipped for the great works they are called to do in
his name. They may ask anything of him in that mission and
they will receive it.

Stephen, the first martyr, and the multitude of martyrs who
have followed — more in the twentieth century than in any
other — received the courage to face what befell them, tragic as
it was. For most of us, martyrdom is found in our grace-given
unavoidable sensitivity and empathy, our inability to walk away.
In prayer, in preaching, in pastoral practice, and in political
action we take into ourselves the negative energies of the world's
injustice, embracing them through the strength of our gospel
hope even as we rage and weep. God is with us: "Do not let
your hearts be troubled."

To still our hearts and rekindle our hope as a community of
faith, God gives us moments in which we glimpse the future in
the present, *proleptic* moments, which afford a vision of hope
fulfilled. Sometimes it is a personal experience with revelatory
power such as my chance meeting with the Deer Creek rabbits.
The exquisite joy of reconciliation and healing in a family torn
apart and now made whole is a visit of God's reign when all

will be reconciled. Such proleptic moments remind us of the faithfulness of God's promise.

In fact, the Bible is crammed full of promises. In Matthew 16:18, in response to Peter's confession of Jesus as the Messiah, Jesus promises that he will build his church on the faith of Peter's witness, and "the gates of Hades will not prevail against it." The gates of hell will assail but they will not prevail. Evil will take its toll, but God's mission will go on unabated.[3]

Fascism, communism, and other forms of political tyranny have vowed to bury the church and have killed and tortured its leaders throughout the ages and throughout the world. But the tyrannies of the world have come and gone, and still the faith remains. When the wall fell in Berlin, it was the church, like Joshua and his tiny band, who brought it down with the trumpet of faith. Within hours of communism's defeat in Romania, people were reported singing Christmas carols in the streets of Bucharest.

The secularism of our modern era has threatened to push the church and its message and mission to the margins of society, seeking to make it irrelevant, perhaps not even worth persecuting. Secularism denies transcendence. It elevates reason and science as the sure path of knowledge, which has emancipated us from the religious superstitions and authority of a less enlightened past. Unlike the violent assaults of the persecutors, the assault of secularism on the church is one of arrogant, yawning bemusement. However, the secularist dream of all-sufficient reason is dying the ignominious death of simple failure. It has not produced a universal set of values by which we can all live or even effectively adjudicated the differences among us. It has not produced communities in which we can grow. It has not produced justice by which we can govern with equity. It has not provided peace by which we can survive. It has not produced clean air for us to breathe. So today, at the end of our millennium, we find a sudden wellspring of hunger for spiritual guidance, power, and renewal.

Certainly racism, sexism, and classism have threatened the promised equality of the reign of God, which the church proclaims. As we have seen earlier, these "isms" bedevil the church itself, creating a weakness in its witness. Yet, God has raised up for us leaders like Martin Luther King, Jr., Dag Hammarskjöld, Mother Teresa, Oscar Romero, Nelson Mandela, and Desmond Tutu. These faithful ones have helped to lead us out of our own captivity to prejudice to renewal in the church and a revitalized witness for justice in society.

All these, people and events, have been the appearance of the future in the midst of the present. They are a continual reminder that the promise is true: The gates of Hades will not prevail against the church and God's mission. "Do not let your hearts be troubled." You who mourn will be comforted.

IN THE MEANTIME

Proleptic moments are, after all, proleptic. They remind us of the promised future but also that the future is future. We live the in-between time, the not-yet time, in the meantime. We live by faith and hope and not yet by sight. We live a "yes" and "no" existence, proleptic moments standing in contrast to the often grim reality of the present moments.

We grieve over so many children who never have a chance to grow and be healthy, even as we rejoice over those who are strong in faith and life with opportunities never before seen on earth. My own children have had unprecedented health care and educational possibilities. Yet, there are countless children in our own country without health care, growing up under poisonous conditions in substandard schools. In the poor country of Tanzania, East Africa, parents now have to pay for their children's education at every level.

This is such a hardship that many children will predictably never finish their education. Moreover, the shortage of funds inevitably compromises what education is delivered. As I was walking down a dusty road in that country, I was suddenly met by a flock of schoolchildren on their way home. It was only eleven o'clock in the morning. How could this be? I asked a local resident. She explained that often the teachers don't show up or cannot stay the whole day, so the children are set free. We live "in the meantime."

We experience the thrill of those who emerge out of the darkness of alienation into the bright light of reconciliation, even as we know there are some who never make it back home. One day I talked with a father whose daughter had ended years of estrangement and again accepted his love even as she offered hers. He recounted some precious incidents that embodied their reborn life together. Tears of gladness filled his eyes. The very next day, sitting in the barber chair, I was told of a young woman who wanted her dad to walk her down the aisle for her wedding. She was his only daughter. However, sadly, her mother, who was divorced from her father, was still so embittered that she refused to be at her daughter's wedding if the father was there too. We live in the in-between time.

We rejoice that Hitler's Holocaust is a thing of the past. We raise monuments and build museums to remember that event so that it can never happen again. We tell stories of heroic efforts by persons of conscience to save the Jews in order to remind ourselves that goodness can assert itself even in the face of colossal evil. Yet even as we do these things, there is a new holocaust under way in the ethnic cleansing of the Balkans. We live in the "not-yet" world.

We rejoice that the civil rights movement has gained us greater equality and opened doors to millions, doors that were once shut. Yet, at the same time we lament the new forms that racism takes and new outbreaks of hate crimes. All over our cities and suburbs we can find neighborhoods that are almost like little global villages. They display a cultural diversity unthinkable a generation ago. Yet, as I write this two men are being tried for the dragging death of a black man, just out of racist hate, and two others are being tried for the brutal beating death of a young gay man, just out of hate. Another man, a white supremacist, is awaiting trial for killing an Asian-American postman and opening fire on women and children at a Jewish community center. We live "in the meantime." We have seen the transfiguration of all life in the glow of the mountain, but we are called for the time being to preach justice in the dim light of the plain.

In a real sense, we cannot conclude this discussion, only this

little book. The call to preach justice continues until the fulfillment of history. However, a last word for this space must be
crafted. For that purpose I'd like to call on my teacher Joseph
Sittler one final time. His comments are, as usual, eloquent and
they seem suitable. His words are a reflection on the life of faith
in the in-between time and to these he adds those of W. H. Au-
den's Christmas oratorio, "For the Time Being," itself a poem
of the not-yet world.

> The place of grace must be in the webbed connectedness
> of man's creaturely life. That web does not indeed be-
> stow grace; it is necessarily the theatre for that anguish
> and delight, that maturation of longing and hope, that
> solidification of knowledge that can attain. As regards ul-
> timate issues, not a clean, crisp certainty but rather the
> knowledge that:
>
> > We who must die demand a miracle.
> > How could the Eternal do a temporal act,
> > The Infinite become a finite fact?
> > Nothing can save us that is possible;
> > We who must die demand a miracle.[4]

As we pursue the cause of justice in the "webbed connect-
edness" of our creaturely life, seeking the grace of God for the
anguish of humankind and the wounded body of nature, we
do so knowing that in the Christmas incarnation the Eternal
did do a temporal act and the infinite did become a finite fact.
In Easter the impossible *has* happened. We who must die have
our miracle.

NOTES

Chapter One

1. H. Richard Niebuhr, *Christ and Culture* (New York: Harper and Row, 1951), 1–2.
2. See the discussion in Glen H. Stassen, D. M. Yeager, and John Howard Yoder, *Authentic Transformation: A New Vision of Christ and Culture* (Nashville: Abingdon, 1996), especially the essay by Yoder.
3. Ibid., 45–82.
4. Ibid., 51–55.
5. Ibid., 99.
6. Ibid., 170–85.
7. Quoted in Karl Hertz, ed., *Two Kingdoms and One World* (Minneapolis: Augsburg, 1976), 83–84.
8. Ulrich Duchrow, ed., *Lutheran Churches: Salt or Mirror of Society?* (Geneva: Lutheran World Federation, 1977), 12. I have further developed this discussion of Lutheran two-realms thought in "Ethics and the Promise of God" in *The Promise of Lutheran Ethics*, ed. Karen L. Bloomquist and John R. Stumme (Minneapolis: Fortress Press, 1998), 98–104.
9. George F. Thomas, *Christian Ethics and Moral Philosophy* (New York: Scribner's, 1955), 246–61.
10. Ibid., 256–61. See also Reinhold Niebuhr, *An Interpretation of Christian Ethics* (New York: Harpers, 1935), chapter 4.
11. See Paul Tillich, "The Protestant Principle and the Proletarian Situation" in *The Protestant Era* (Chicago: The University of Chicago Press, 1957), 165–70. Also, *Systematic Theology*, vol. 3 (Chicago: The University of Chicago Press, 1951), 355–56.
12. Joseph Sittler, *The Structure of Christian Ethics* (Baton Rouge: Louisiana State University Press, 1958).
13. See George Hunsinger, "Toward a Radical Barth" in George Hunsinger, ed., *Karl Barth And Radical Politics* (Philadelphia: Westminster, 1976), 223–25.
14. Barend de Vries, *Champions of the Poor* (Washington, D.C.: Georgetown University Press, 1998), 206.
15. Ibid., 218.
16. Ibid., 219.
17. "Give Us this Day Our Daily Bread: Sufficient Sustainable Livelihood

103

for All" (Chicago: Division for Church and Society, Evangelical Lutheran Church in America: October 1996), 19.

18. Quoted in Larry L. Rasmussen, *Moral Fragments and Moral Community* (Minneapolis: Fortress Press, 1993), 103.

19. Ibid., 104.

20. Joseph A. Sittler, *Gravity and Grace,* ed. Linda-Marie Delloff (Minneapolis: Augsburg, 1986), 35.

21. J. Philip Wogaman, *Speaking the Truth in Love: Prophetic Preaching to a Broken World* (Louisville: Westminster John Knox, 1998), 16.

22. First I want to acknowledge my debt to these theologians and their most prominent American counterpart, my teacher, Carl Braaten. Their work is so vast that it is hard to pick one source for this key point. Certainly the landmark volume for Moltmann would have to be his early work, *Theology of Hope,* trans. James W. Leitch (New York: Harper and Row, 1967), and for Pannenberg, *Jesus — God and Man,* trans. Lewis Wilkens and Duane A. Priebe (Philadelphia: Westminster, 1968). However, both Moltmann and Pannenberg continue to be productive to this date.

23. Nile Harper, *Urban Churches Vital Signs: Beyond Charity toward Justice* (Grand Rapids: Eerdmans, 1999), 223–34.

24. Ibid., 230.

25. Ibid., 223.

Chapter Two

1. J. Philip Wogaman, *Speaking the Truth in Love,* 8.

2. Emil Brunner, *Man in Revolt: A Christian Anthropology,* trans. Olive Wyon (Philadelphia: Westminster, 1947), 67.

3. John Milic Lochman, *Signposts to Freedom,* trans. David Lewis (Minneapolis: Augsburg, 1983), 18–20.

4. Robert A. Guelich, *The Sermon on the Mount* (Waco, Texas: Word Books, 1982), 67.

5. See the article on "Natural Law" in *The Westminster Dictionary of Christian Ethics,* ed. James F. Childress and John Macquarrie (Philadelphia: Westminster, 1986). For a typical and more extensive example of how Reformation theology has attacked the natural law tradition, see Helmut Thielicke, *Theological Ethics,* vol. 1, trans. and ed. William Lazareth (Philadelphia: Fortress Press, 1966).

6. Paul Althaus, *The Ethics of Martin Luther,* trans. Robert C. Shultz (Philadelphia: Fortress Press, 1965), 25ff.

7. Articles IV, 22–24 and XX, 9–10.

8. Althaus, *Ethics of Martin Luther,* 27–28.

9. Paul Tillich, *Dynamics of Faith* (New York: Harper and Brothers, 1957), 1–29.

10. George W. Forell, *The Augsburg Confession: A Contemporary Commentary* (Minneapolis: Augsburg, 1968), 35–36.

11. Joseph A Sittler, *Grace Notes and Other Fragments*, ed. Robert M. Herhold and Linda Marie Delloff (Philadelphia: Fortress Press, 1981), 77–78.

12. Thielicke, *Theological Ethics*, vol. 1, 496.

Chapter Three

1. James H. Cone, "The White Church and Black Power" in *Black Theology: A Documentary History, 1966–79*, ed. Gayraud S. Wilmore and James H. Cone (Maryknoll, N.Y.: Orbis Books, 1979), 126–29. This chapter was reprinted from James H. Cone, *Black Theology and Black Power* (New York: Seabury Press, 1969).

2. Ibid., 128.

3. James H. Cone, *God of the Oppressed* (New York: Seabury Press, 1975), 15.

4. Cain Hope Felder, ed., *Stony the Road We Trod* (Minneapolis: Fortress Press, 1991), 2–8.

5. Derrick Bell, *Faces at the Bottom of the Well* (New York: Basic Books, 1992), 9–10.

6. Ibid., 150–57.

7. Georgie Anne Geyer, "The President's Initiative Goes Nowhere," *The Columbus Dispatch* (June 29, 1999), 7A.

8. Reinhold Niebuhr, *Man's Nature and His Communities* (New York: Charles Scribner's Sons, 1965), 90–91.

9. Cornel West, *Keeping Faith: Philosophy and Race in America* (New York and London: Routledge, 1993), 268–70.

10. Ibid., xviii.

11. Ibid., 29, 291. See also Cornel West, *Race Matters* (Boston: Beacon Press, 1993), 63–67.

12. Samuel B. McKinney, "The Hot Winds of Change" in William M. Philpot, ed., *Best Black Sermons* (Valley Forge, Pa.: Judson Press, 1972), 46.

13. Harper, *Urban Churches, Vital Signs*, 143.

14. Ted Peters, *God — The World's Future* (Minneapolis: Fortress Press, 1992), 297.

15. James Evans, Jr. *We Shall All Be Changed* (Minneapolis: Fortress Press, 1997), 40–41.

16. Benjamin E. Mays, "What Man Lives By," *Best Black Sermons*, 35–36.

17. Robert Michael Franklin, "Church and City: African American Christianity's Ministry" in Eleanor Scott Meyers, ed., *Envisioning a New City* (Louisville: Westminster John Knox, 1992), 146.

18. Ibid., 147.

Chapter Four

1. William Raspberry, "School Killings Illustrate Black-White Gulf," *The Columbus Post-Dispatch* (May 7, 1999), 13A.

2. Ibid.

3. D. E. King, "The God Who Takes Off Chariot Wheels," *Best Black Sermons*, 27.

4. Crispin Sartwell, *Act Like You Know: African-American Autobiography and White Identity* (Chicago and London: University of Chicago Press, 1998), 55–60.

5. As quoted in ibid., 60.

6. A report of this conference with selected papers was published in *Word and World*, 7, 1 (Winter 1987), 6–90.

7. Quoted in Mark Thompson, "On Relating Justice and Justification," *Word and World*, 7, 1 (Winter 1987), 9.

8. The quotes that follow come from Ernesto Cardenal, *The Gospel in Solentiname*, vol. 1, trans. Donald D. Walsh (Maryknoll, N.Y.: Orbis Books, 1976), 141–47.

9. David A. Farmer and Edwina Hunter, eds., *And Blessed Is She: Sermons by Women* (New York: Harper & Row, 1990), 94–95.

10. Christine M. Smith, *Weaving the Sermon: Preaching in a Feminist Perspective* (Louisville: Westminster John Knox, 1989), 19.

11. Ibid., 114, 128.

12. In Farmer and Hunter, eds., *And Blessed Is She*, 191.

13. Ibid., 147.

14. Olin P. Moyd, *The Sacred Art: Preaching and Theology in the African American Tradition* (Valley Forge, Pa.: Judson Press, 1995), 85–86.

15. Henry H. Mitchell, *Black Preaching: The Recovery of a Powerful Art* (Nashville: Abingdon Press, 1990), 127–29.

16. Robert M. Simmons, *Good Religion: Expressions of Energy in Traditional African-American Religion* (Columbus: Layman Christian Leadership Publication, 1998), 50.

17. Joseph A. Sittler, *Essays on Nature and Grace* (Philadelphia: Fortress Press, 1972), 52–73.

18. Simmons, *Good Religion*, 57.

19. Tillich, *Dynamics of Faith*, 30–40.

Chapter Five

1. Wogaman, *Speaking the Truth in Love*, 61.

2. James M. Childs, Jr., *Ethics in Business: Faith at Work* (Minneapolis: Fortress Press, 1995), 8–10.

3. See, for example, Richard T. DeGeorge, *Business Ethics*, 3d ed. (New York: Macmillan, 1990), 163–64; and Heidi Vernon, *Business and Society: A Managerial Approach*, 6th ed. (New York: McGraw-Hill, 1998), 88.

4. R. Edward Freeman and Jeanne Liedka, "Corporate Social Responsibility: A Critical Approach," *Business Horizons* (July–August 1991), 92–98, cited in Vernon, *Business and Society*, 27–28.

5. John Kenneth Galbraith, *The Affluent Society* (Boston: Houghton-Mifflin, 1958), 78–97.

6. Vernon, *Business and Society*, 7.

7. I have published an extensive ethical reflection on the problem of greed entitled *Greed: Economics and Ethics in Conflict* (Minneapolis: Fortress Press, 2000). While this brief chapter takes a somewhat different approach and makes use of some fresh material, it is also reflective of the discussion in the book and makes use of a few of its references.

8. Stanley Hauerwas with Richard Dondi and David Burrell, *Truth, Fullness and Tragedy* (Notre Dame: University of Notre Dame Press, 1977) and Stanley Hauerwas, *A Community of Character* (Notre Dame: University of Notre Dame Press, 1981). Alasdair MacIntyre, *After Virtue* (Notre Dame: University of Notre Dame Press, 1981).

9. Roger G. Betsworth, *Social Ethics: An Examination of American Moral Traditions* (Louisville: Westminster John Knox, 1990), 53.

10. Ibid., 58–73.

11. Andrew Carnegie, *The Gospel of Wealth and Other Timely Essays* (Cambridge, Mass.: Belknap Press of Harvard University Press, 1962), 16–17. The original article, "The Gospel of Wealth" was published in 1889.

12. Betsworth, *Social Ethics*, 80.

13. Carnegie, *The Gospel of Wealth*, 19.

14. Betsworth, *Social Ethics*, 79.

15. On this as a parable of eschatological reversal, see Walter Pilgrim, *Good News for the Poor: Wealth and Poverty in Luke-Acts* (Minneapolis: Augsburg, 1981), 106.

16. Douglas John Hall, *The Steward: A Biblical Symbol Come of Age*, rev. ed. (Grand Rapids: Eerdmans, 1990), 12–16, 167.

17. Harper, *Urban Churches*, 171.

18. Ibid., 174.

19. Ibid., 172.

20. Thomas L. Friedman, "Face It, This Nation Is a Hyperpower," *Columbus Dispatch* (Sunday, April 22, 1999), 3B.

Chapter Six

1. John L. Kater, Jr., "Faithful Church, Plural World: Diversity at Lambeth," *Anglican Theological Review*, 81, 2 (Spring 1999), 246–47.

2. The text of Mr. Wolfensohn's address was made available on the internet via Worldwide Faith News, www.wfn.org, on July 25, 1998.

3. Ibid.

4. Richard Lischer, "Preaching as the Church's Language" in *Listening to the Word*, ed. Gail R. O'Day and Thomas G. Long (Nashville: Abingdon, 1993), 115.

5. H. Paul Santmire, *The Travail of Nature: The Ambiguous Ecological Promise of Christian Theology* (Philadelphia: Fortress Press, 1985), 175–82, provides a terse summary of his historical research.

6. John Passacantando, "Drought, Hurricanes Prove There's a Big Change in the Weather," and H. Sterling Burnett, "Major Scientists Say It's a Figment of Gore's Imagination," *Columbus Dispatch* (September 4, 1999), 10A.

7. Santmire, *Travail of Nature,* 197.

8. See for example, James A. Nash, *Loving Nature: Ecological Integrity and Christian Responsibility* (Nashville: Abingdon, 1991), 102–3.

9. Gerhard von Rad, *Genesis,* trans. John H. Marks (Philadelphia: Westminster, 1961), 57–58.

10. Reinhold Niebuhr, *The Nature and Destiny of Man,* vol. 1 (New York: Charles Scribner's Sons, 1949), 190–91, quoted in Nash, *Loving Nature,* 121.

11. Larry L. Rasmussen, *Earth Community Earth Ethics* (Maryknoll, N.Y.: Orbis Books, 1996), 258–59.

12. Ibid., 230–42.

13. *Keeping and Healing the Creation* (Louisville: Committee on Social Witness Policy, Presbyterian Church [U.S.A.], 1989); the discussion of the norms I cite is contained in chapter 5, 61–81.

14. Ibid., 63.

Chapter Seven

1. For a discussion of the Beatitudes as gifts of grace brought in with Jesus' revelation of the reign of God, see my book *Faith, Formation, and Decision: Ethics in the Community of Promise* (Minneapolis: Fortress Press, 1992), 35ff.

2. Henri J. M. Nouwen, *The Wounded Healer: Ministry in Contemporary Society* (Garden City, N.Y.: Doubleday, 1972), 90.

3. Many of the thoughts that follow in this section first appeared in a sermon I preached on the occasion of the Week of Prayer for Christian Unity. It was published under the editor's title, "The Secularist Dream is Dying," in *Josephinum Journal of Theology,* 3, 1 (Winter/Spring 1996), 4–7.

4. Sittler, *Essays on Nature and Grace,* 94.

INDEX